Turn Out THE Lights

Memorable Plays and Short Stories for the Screen

LAURA LONSHEIN LUDWIG

Library of Congress Control Number: 2024914808

ISBN
978-1-964982-29-8 (Paperback)
978-1-964982-30-4 (eBook)
978-1-964982-28-1 (Hardcover)

Dedication

For Professor Patricia Law Ormandy and
Ad Augeri, a singer-songwriter

TABLE OF CONTENTS

SCREEN AND STAGE PLAYS

France in the Art Movement

Written on August 2012

The play opens in the year 1887 in the painter Lautrec's apartment in France. Lautrec is a man who is affected for life by two accidents that took place earlier in his life. His legs are stunted, his upper body is heavier, and his head is huge. He has a black beard and a large nose and mouth. He is noble, kind, and he understands life is not fair and must be lived to the fullest.

LAUTREC (*talks warmly without a trace of snobbery to his servant*). Tonight is the Courier Francais Fe'te. We will show this fool—this man who loves to kill joy, Senator Berenger—how life is lived.

MAID (*speaks to Lautrec with affection and respect*). Will you be wearing a costume to this ball?

LAUTREC. Of course I will. I will be dressed as a lithographer's apprentice or a choirboy.

MAID. That's marvelous.

Scene moves to a woman reading a French newspaper in the street with a friend standing next to her.

WOMAN (*reads to herself*). Henri de Toulouse-Lautrec-Monfa… (*Stops reading to herself.*) Look at the Society page, Rene. I'll read it to you. The artists will be giving Senator Berenger the time of his life at a ball with wine flowing and that wild dance they do—you know, the quadrille. That artist Lautrec will attend. (*Looks at her friend, stops reading.*) His ancestry goes back to the royal family. I believe a prince was in his family. Odd-looking. He makes the best of things though, a merry fellow I hear.

The scene shifts to the ball. An orchestra can be seen playing French tunes of the period. Dancers could be seen, some in acrobatic gyrations, most doing the quadrille in an accomplished manner (the cancan, as it is known to Americans). Wine is on every table, and people are laughing gaily, some telling funny tales.

LAUTREC. (Lautrec is dressed as a choirboy, seated at a table with Aristide Bruant. Lautrec is sketching on an artist's pad. He is drawing the people at the party and Aristide. He has a sketch pad of himself as well.) I think I have this one the way I want it.

(Shows the picture to Aris tide.)

ARISTIDE BRUANT. (*Aristide is dressed as a saint. Aristide looks at the people sitting next to them in the costumes in the drawing. He speaks to Lautrec.*) Yes, that's very good. That man in the Japanese costume and the lady with him, interesting costume she's wearing.

At the table next to Lautrec and Aristide, the woman gets up quickly and walks to a friend standing nearby. The man in the Japanese costume sits, looking at her as she speaks to him. Neither seems aware that a picture was drawn of them.

LAUTREC. See how time changes everything. In another minute, I would not have had it.

ARISTIDE (nods his head in agreement and speaks to Lautrec). Yes.

The camera or stage direction shifts to some men dressed in top hats, talking and drinking wine, and then to the stage where there is a line of women dancing. Swirling petticoats can be seen, their legs pointing skyward. People can be seen talking and laughing across the room from Lautrec and Aristide.

Hours later at the ball, everyone is gone. Only fig leaves can be seen.

WAITER (*clearing the table, talking to himself*). How the people carry on. They shed their clothes and only fig leafs can be seen.

Note to the director: The author, Ms. Ludwig, does not want any nudity in this film or stage play.

In the next act of the play or scene in the film, it is the year 1889 at the Moulin Rouge, a resort and showplace that competed with the others and became the most popular. A sign is being taken down since this resort is now bought by another man, Monsieur Chauvin, who is putting up a new sign: Le Trianon.

CHAUVIN (*talking to a friend*). I will make this a greater place to see—a theater, dance hall, and café. Concerts, light opera, and sometimes, for the intellectuals, a few lectures. A new pavilion for dancing.

FRIEND. It should be great.

The scene shifts to an earlier night, in a dark spot away from the main street in 1888 at the Moulin Rouge, a favorite spot of Lautrec. The building was not a real windmill. On the roof of the Moulin Rouge is a painted windmill. Lautrec is seated at his reserved table. A happy crowd of people talk at tables. Lively music and witty songs are sung. The lighting is good enough at the Moulin Rouge to draw pictures, which Lautrec often does. The walls are red, covered with photographs and posters. There is a large ballroom where the dancers dance, which looks like it was a railway station. The director of the Moulin Rouge, who got all the dancers together, is seen talking to the dancers, not far from Lautrec's table. La Goulue is one of the dancers. She is dressed in black silk stockings, one foot shoed in black satin.

CHARLES ZIDLER (*director at the Moulin Rouge, talks to the dancers*). Are you ready to thrill them tonight?

LA GOULUE (a feisty woman speaking with a happy, defiant air at the world, smiles respectfully at Zidler). As always.

VALENTIN LE DÉSOSSÉ (*a man somewhat gentle in manner*). We will dance together, La Goulue.

LA GOULUE (*in a loving, friendly way*). Of course, Valentin.

La Goulue is voluptuously built. She sways her hips as she picks up the wine glasses of the people at their seats at the tables she passes. The people look at her in a friendly way. As she passes, she speaks to a handsome man who is with his girlfriend at a table.

LA GOULUE. Ready to see me dance?

MAN AT A TABLE (*speaks to La Goulue*). I sure am.

WOMAN SEATED AT THE TABLE (smiles in a friendly and fun manner).

La Goulue dances on the stage. Her blond hair is styled with a ringlet of hair hanging to her eyebrows, and the rest is piled on to her head. She is attractive in a hard way. She has shapely legs, with lace falling to her ankles. Knots of pink ribbon can be seen at her knees. She has yards of lace on her petticoat. As she dances, it swirls. One can see a heart embroidered on her underpants. Her skirt is black.

VALENTIN (dances with La Goulue)

Valentin and La Goulue are dancing on the stage. Valentin is a highly accomplished dancer—agile, with perfect muscle control. He seems to be made of rubber. He dances with La Goulue as a partner. Valentin is dressed in a rusty-black frock coat and a silk hat, tipped over his eyes at a severe angle. He dances without romance in a professional manner. She is his admiring pupil always. He is very thin, sunken eyes half-closed, thin unsmiling lips.

The camera or stage scene moves to the table where Lautrec is seated, watching La Goulue and Valentin dancing at this show. Lautrec is drawing a picture of the dancers. La Goulue is seen in the drawing in her childlike delight of dancing, as well as some of her more impulsive, cruel expressions in the style that Lautrec was famous for.

Lautrec, the painter, and the painter Vincent van Gogh are seated at this table together, discussing art.

LAUTREC. I love drawing the dancers.

VINCENT VAN GOGH. It is wonderful to be here. This is much more encouraging to me than any other place I've been to.

LAUTREC. You can find comfort here. Your life as an artist is appreciated.

VINCENT VAN GOGH. I don't like art classes. I never fit in to any of them. Aside from that, I am happier here. In Paris, I love walking along the boulevard. The cafes and cabarets inspire me. The cafes are filled with life. I am in a nice apartment now.

LAUTREC. Remember the showing at the Salon des Indépendants in March of 1888? It was earlier this year.

VINCENT VAN GOGH. Of course I do. I would like to show *Starry Night Over the Rhone* at the next one. The critics mean nothing to me, and they mean nothing to you, am I right?

LAUTREC. I never care what people say. I have had to live my life the way I want to despite people telling me what to do all my life. They could not possibly understand why I do the things I do. They have only the experience of getting up each day with a plan that will work because they are what people will call the trustworthy, easy-to-understand man. They look at art the way people want them to.

VINCENT VAN GOGH. But we both know they are anything but trustworthy. I have learned that people are not what they seem.

LAUTREC. That is true. In art, there are those painters who have inspired me. You are, of course, one of the most independent and inventive artists I know. Your use of color is unique. Vincent, I have also studied Ingres, Daumier, and Degas. I am inspired by the use of lines in the Japanese artists I have seen.

VINCENT VAN GOGH. I admire the work of Rubens, Eugene Delacroix, his use of color. The work of Millet is challenging.

LAUTREC. Yes, Millet is concerned with history.

VINCENT VAN GOGH. I have painted so much more here than I have ever painted before. Two hundred and thirty pictures in two years in Paris. The roofs of Paris from the heights of Montmartre street scenes fascinate me. The places people love to see—the Pont du Carrousel, the Jardin du Luxembourg, the Bois de Boulogne, where people dressed in fashionable clothes walk or ride in a very cheerful spot. Montmartre, outside Paris, where you love to paint, I have also enjoyed working in. I painted the *Sloping Path in Montmartre* in 1886, a recent work. It was a little before it had lost the village atmosphere, and a street scene, Le Moulin a Poivre, in 1887, and a few surviving windmills, the Moulin de La Galette, without the dance halls in the paintings.

LAUTREC. Well, the nightlife—I will always be the one to paint that.

The camera or stage scene returns to the dancers in the room. And since the quadrille is always danced by four people, the partners that La Goulue and Valentin select are a man named Guibollard and a woman known by the name Grille d' Egout, which means "sewer grating." She can be seen as a good-natured person with a smile that exposes two teeth, rodent-like and long, which project over her lower lip. Though she does not use foul language and La Goulue does. Grille d' Egout can be charming and modest, but when in the dance, she will also kick a man's hat off his head and pirouette on her toes, exposing thin, attractive legs, invent variations of the dance, and keep in time with the music—all of which she does in this scene.

GRILLE D' EGOUT (dances the quadrille with La Goulue and Valentin).

GUIBOLLARD (dances the quadrille with Valentin, La Goulue, and Grille d' E gout).

The camera or stage scene returns to the table where Vincent van Gogh and Lautrec are seated.

VINCENT VAN GOGH (*speaks to Lautrec*). I wonder if we will be remembered as that great writer Victor Hugo was. He died a few years ago, and they say over a million people followed the procession.

LAUTREC (*responds to Vincent van Gogh*). People say Victor Hugo is the greatest writer in France. He wrote *Les Miserables*. It is believed that he will be remembered for a long time.

VINCENT VAN GOGH. Gustave Flaubert has suffered for the truth.

Enter Paul Gaugin, the painter. He walks to the table where Lautrec and Vincent van Gogh are seated.

PAUL GAUGIN. May I join you?

VINCENT VAN GOGH. Please do.

LAUTREC. Yes, of course.

VINCENT VAN GOGH. We were just talking about the great writers in France, the hard life the dedicated artists live, and the importance of literature to us.

PAUL GAUGIN. Yes, I have enjoyed reading great works of literature. The literature of the eighteenth century was dominated by philosophers such as Voltaire and Jean-Jacques Rousseau. I remember my first year in Paris in 1876, when I began to devote myself more fully to art. Zola was unknown to me then. I believe *L'Assommoir* was not published at that time. Zola later defended the impressionists. He said of painting, "Art was a fragment of nature seen through temperament." One must have the personal life needed to be an artist. That is an important fact about artists. I admire Monet and Renoir. In the year 1869, Monet was so poor that Renoir had to bring bread from his home or he would have died of hunger. The poor artist struggled for the sake of beauty, discovering the desire to build life through what his path offered to him—sights, sounds, and insights. Unfortunately, that is not the definition of life for everyone. In Europe, money is a bridge between men and women, not art. The women in my family were of a greater heritage. My mother loved to read. My grandmother was a well-known and much loved lady. She spent her entire fortune in the workers' cause and the Workers' Union. The workers set up a monument to her in the cemetery of Bordeaux. She was a socialist. Many delegations followed her coffin. I was told she was a genius. My mother, her daughter, was brought up in a school. My mother was a very noble Spanish lady. We shared many delightful conversations about literature. My father set out for Lima. He was a political correspondent and wanted to start a newspaper. He died on the ship—a strange problem with the captain. We were left poor, an entire fortune lost. I have had to work hard all my life. When I was beginning to speak French, I was first in the habit of speaking Spanish. I was thinking about what I would do to find the great and beautiful experiences in life when so many people refuse to care about the truth. The truth is what you feel, not what you are told to feel. It is a lifetime search to free yourself from imposed beliefs and live the life you want and need to live.

LAUTREC. Yes, that is what is wrong and has always been the problem with what people set up as the most important rules to follow.

VINCENT VAN GOGH. The truth is in the divine experience. Painting and literature are the most important experiences in life. The most necessary.

LAUTREC. There will always be those that wish to silence artists that speak the truth. The feelings that are expressed because of the time one lives in moves the spirit in mankind to a new reflection, and those that are threatened by it work at destroying the ways that the artist can reach the people. Intellectuals suffer all the time.

The cure for Rousseau was a more authentic civilization. There is nothing permanent in civilization, but not because people need change and must experience what a new century has to offer. People need security—sometimes at any cost. The only exception is under a brutal dictator. Then you might find the average person seeks change to avoid the misery he would suffer for his entire life without change. The adventurer, the artist, or intellectual must see what is unfolding. And peeking through, almost through time, they need to create what they experience. In the worst of times, the structure or inflexible arrangement is put in place by those that make the most money and protected with armed force, often to destroy the writer, philosopher, painter, and teacher. Time will reveal to us, since we are still in the infancy of our inventions, as to whether what will be used and bought by the buyer will give pleasure to the senses man possesses or enslaves him. The balance of power has always been the problem. My family has been at war with one another for over a hundred years.

VINCENT VAN GOGH. I believe mankind must question who he is. What is our purpose in regard to one another? Look at what I lived through. Those that demanded I deliver sermons serve the people and, at the same time, control my love of mankind and stifle my will to offer mercy. Why is mankind unable to control the tide? A dark age is continually threatening a renaissance. Berthe Morisot, you know—Degas helped her to gain confidence. She was a great painter, but a woman. Because she is a woman, she cannot sit at this table with us and discuss art. She cannot go to dinner at a café by herself. If her father was a poor man instead of a rich man, she never would have been able to study in Paris. She would be working in a factory or cleaning the house for a family. Although she is a wealthy woman, she cannot discuss world affairs with anyone but her close friends in her parlor.

PAUL GAUGIN. I am going to build a better life. I believe a paradise can be found.

LAUTREC. Be careful wherever you go. There is always something to look out for. I suppose, in the future, we will find out how to hold on to a paradise.

The End

THE WINTER

February 2010

This is a play. It could be a stage or screenplay. The directing should be brilliant with attention to the inner life of the actors through the type of work one would find in the earlier Ingmar Bergman films. If it is a screenplay, attention to the body and face as an artistic guide that one would find in the best works of black-and-white photography, body stance, and work in bringing to the set those objects around the actor that enhance both the message and the beauty of the scene, with careful attention to those objects such as the bed, chair, coffee table, and curtains. The camera work should make art the rule in working with light, shadows, and darkness. Fade-outs should occur with precision. The exterior shots should demonstrate an understanding of the possibilities that can be captured as found in the best works of the Swedish and German films in the more experimental and highly mindful periods of art prior to the early 1970s—when films took a turn for action with less respect for the art and more of a desire to simply bring action to the screen too continuously. There are no nude sex scenes in this work, and suggestions of sexual encounters should allow the actor the best opportunity to use acting as the means to project the desire.

THE MAN. (No lines, just stares at the sky.)

A man silently stares at the sky. He is a hungry-looking, thin, pale, tired man with deeply set brown eyes, oval in shape. He looks up at the sky. He is wearing slightly baggy blue jeans and a white jacket, not suited for the winter weather. He has thinning brown hair.

The camera moves to his face, a strong close-up, as he looks at the sky and then moves his body slowly. He is walking on a road.

The camera moves to capture the sky, which is white without a trace of color. Snow is falling, and it has been three days without fail. One of the longest snowstorms to hit the state of New York.

The camera moves to a farmhouse, to a living room with a small coffee table in unvarnished wood. A book rests on the table. It is on the life and work of Ingmar Bergman. No one can be seen in the room.

The camera then moves to another house, to a room with only a sofa and coffee table. A young woman is holding a baby in her arms, standing very straight, and looking concerned. No one else is in the room. She is wearing a light purple dress, which oddly looks like a 1940s-style dress. It is a plain dress but falls against the body in a somewhat seductive manner. This seems to happen naturally, as she wears no makeup and her hair is plainly drawn back in a ponytail.

The camera enters another house. A beautiful woman is drinking a cup of coffee in a kitchen alone. The kitchen has a large modern refrigerator, a table, two chairs, and chrome legs on the table and chairs. She is counting money, which she takes from a canister with the word *flour* on it. The woman recounts the money several times. A close-up of the money in her hands and the counting action.

A man enters the kitchen in a shirt and good sports pants.

KAREN (*to the man*). When will we have the money to go to Europe? To do the types of things we waited years to do? Just enough to buy food and the necessary things.

JOHN. It's been snowing for days. We're lucky we can buy food.

KAREN. It's God's own judgment on so punishing a place where only thieves prosper.

JOHN. I did the best I could. What have you done to make it better?

KAREN. I could do something for us, but I doubt it will be easy. It's hard to find a new job that pays well enough to make a difference for a woman over forty.

JOHN. Aren't you happy with what we have?

KAREN. I just want to see more of the world. Perhaps to go to France someday, sit in an outdoor café with you that overlooks a river that looks like a painting by Renoir, dance with you in a nightclub, and walk on a cobblestone street in the moonlight.

JOHN. I would love to do that too. Perhaps someday we will.

John exits the kitchen.

The scene shifts to a snowfall that has continued for four days. The camera captures a road where the snow covers tall trees and houses in upstate New York. The sky is completely white. The camera moves along the road as though someone were driving slowly, but no car or people can be seen. This effect can be achieved on a set if it is done with great care to achieve the appearance of a white sky and a snowfall that covers two or three houses on a road and covers all the trees. The hungry-looking man wearing slightly baggy blue jeans and a white jacket (seen in the beginning of the play on the first page) is there. He is walking on the road, and there is a close-up of his whole body.

THE MAN (*talks to himself*). Perhaps this is what hell looks like. It is cold and the sky is perfectly white. I'll keep walking. It won't be long now. A half mile and I'll be there.

The scene returns to Karen and John's house. John is sitting in the living room. He is sitting on a comfortable chair with a broad back to it. It is a cushioned chair. There is a large bookcase beside the television set, and it has a few classic works in literature, poetry, Hart Crane, Robert Frost. There are books on world history, travel books, and a few mystery novels.

Karen enters the living room and sits on a chair next to him. There is the sound of a fire truck and cars passing. The living-room window faces the road they live on. They live in upstate New York on a road with a few houses on it, a mile from a small town. Karen sits on the chair next to him and begins speaking to him. The camera focuses on Karen and John in close-up shots, alternating between the speaker and listener.

KAREN. I'm sorry, John. I know we need to wait. If you wait for something to happen, it will. If time allows for it, if nothing takes it from you—if floods, poverty, or thieves don't steal it.

JOHN. The whole world is like one large thief. Lies, deceit. Do you know what I wish? I had been a thief myself.

KAREN. It seems foolish to work so hard, to avoid taking what does not belong to you, when everyone takes what should have been ours by keeping us from it. Years of rules, taxes, obligations just to slow us down. Double talk, friends giving opportunities to friends, families helping only their families, and we were always ready to help anyone in need.

JOHN. We could change. I know we can. We could be more like everyone else.

KAREN. We could do better than that. We could take that boss of yours for the ride of a lifetime. We know enough about him to collect close to a million.

JOHN. I see that as justice, nothing more.
    (They hold hands.)

John and Karen move to two chairs near the fireplace in the living room. There is a close-up of the fireplace till only the fireplace can be seen.

The camera moves to the woman seen in the beginning of the play, holding a baby with a concerned expression on her face, silently standing alone. She is still wearing a light purple dress, a 1940s-style dress though it is the twenty-first century. She is young, mid-twenties, and she is now sitting by a window on a rocking chair. The young woman is looking at a photograph of a middle-aged man in his mid-fifties. She is looking at the photograph and speaks to herself, looking at the photo as if it were the person himself.

YOUNG WOMAN. You never loved me. I doubt I loved you. Where are you now? Our child is here with me, and you left me stranded. No money, a rich man, my father's age. I don't know why I did it, and you will never say that the baby is yours. You never told me about your wife.

A close-up of a baby carriage in another part of the room, although a baby cannot be seen in it.

In a new scene, a man is sitting in an expensive restaurant with his wife. He is ordering dinner for them. The waiter, dressed in a light yellow suit, is taking their order. It is a seafood restaurant. The man ordering has gray hair and is handsome. The woman is shapely, pretty, and slightly younger than he is. They are both in their mid-fifties.

DAN. I'll have two glasses of white wine and two shrimp scampi dishes, salad, and we both take Italian dressing, no soup.

EILEEN. Yes, you always know what to order for me. Darling, you know what I like. (*Said to the waiter.*) Nothing else, thank you.

WAITER. Yes, madam, thank you.

EILEEN (*said to her husband*). Is there something wrong, dear? You seem concerned about something.

DAN. No. Nothing is wrong. Nothing now. I feel as though something is going to happen.

The waiter brings the white wine to the table. The camera moves away from them and pans the restaurant, a fireplace, white tablecloths on the tables, candles on the tables, and couples at the tables. People can be seen sitting at the tables, eating, drinking wine, and talking to one another. The camera pans the room, no close-ups, and this scene ends.

The man in slightly baggy pants, blue jeans, and a white jacket can be seen entering a house. He places a key in the lock and enters. It is night, and snow covers the trees on the land. The house sits on a fourth of an acre with a few trees on it. He looks tired and hungry as he did in the last scene. He sits down on an old but uncomfortable armchair after placing his jacket on another chair. It is dark, and there is only one lamp in the room. It is a small desk lamp, and it creates large shadows on the chair. He looks anxious, and he takes a paper from a side table that the lamp rests on and studies it.

THE MAN (*begins to read the letter; he reads to himself out loud*). Your brother will receive most of the money when I die. He worked all his life, never lost a job, and remained married to a responsible woman. I would never leave you stranded. I just don't want you to spend it all at once. John will be responsible for sending you monthly checks.

Scene shifts to Karen and John talking to each other in the kitchen.

KAREN. The question is how we do it. We could find a place far from here, invite him to a dinner party that he would want to go to, and when we have him alone, tell him what we know. No letter, nothing in print. Nothing that can be traced.

JOHN. That's perfect. I need some coffee.

KAREN. Yes, I made a fresh pot, darling.

KAREN. John, I would like to tell you about myself. Once, I did something heroic. I don't want to talk too much about it now, but it never felt good afterwards because it was proven to me that people just wanted me to fail at my goals. My dreams were killed with pleasure, and for years afterwards, by too many people. I want to be remembered as the antihero—a person who will tell the truth. That the theft of my dreams, my time, the beauty I had to offer, the wish to share beautiful ideas, beautiful language, and to save people from the pain I knew was there as a child from a broken home, who once had to live in a group home, my desire to save others appreciated only in childhood makes me not want to play a part. I would like to commit the perfect crime. There is nothing else to do but enjoy life as the antihero to the fullest. Without pretending I was thankful for being kicked for years.

JOHN. Yes, me too. I hope we can do it.

Scene shifts to the living room of a mansion. A plush velvet green sofa, a walnut coffee table, and three paintings—two of ships, large sailboats from the late nineteenth century, and one of a stone house, also from the late nineteenth century. They are not by well-known painters. An elaborate light fixture overhead, and a thick Persian rug covers the floor. It is a large living room with a vase that has the look of the early 1900s. It used to hold flowers in. A thick blue glass vase with no flowers sits on a silver tray on the coffee table. It is the home of Eileen and Dan. The camera lingers on the beautiful furniture in the living room as though someone were walking into the room for the first time.

EILEEN (*speaks to her husband, Dan*). The young woman—you know who I'm talking about—came to see me. I've given my life to you. How could you do this? You're an ugly man, a liar, a cheat, and a deviant man. She's young enough to be your youngest daughter. You lured her in, and when she was pregnant, you left her to suffer and struggle. Maybe they would both die, and you would deny the baby was yours forever! I know when you left me, and the stories you made up matched the details in the stories you told her. And the ones you told her, you would tell me to get away to see her. I'm leaving, and I want half of everything you have. That should easily cover what I'll need.

DAN. I'll give it to you.

EILEEN. I never loved you the way I would have liked to. You always had something about you I wondered about. I could spend a lifetime with you and almost did and never know you. You're a sneaky, self-serving man that is too smooth, too unemotional. Never committed to ideals, no time for philosophy you often said with a disgusted look at me when I had any idea that was too committed to beliefs on the way things should be done.

DAN. Well, you'll have the money. I think it's for the best.

EILEEN. You never loved me, did you?

DAN. I tried. I did the best I could. I cared for you. I think it's best that you have a chance to find someone better, to find happiness. Please just don't tell anyone about it. I'll be ruined in business, and I could never give you anything then. I'll do the right thing by everyone. But I will make sure that you are taken care of and you will never need anything. It will be in writing, and I'll start with a quarter of a million dollars tonight. I have it in my safe.

EILEEN. That suits me, and I don't want to see you again. You'll make the arrangements to make the money available and a quarter of a million tonight. So I could set up somewhere else. I don't want to live in this house.

DAN. You'll have a new house then. I'll give you the money for that too.

A new scene begins, and the camera moves to the home of John and Karen. The thin, pale, tired man who is still wearing baggy blue jeans is the brother of John, Karen's husband. He is seen knocking on John and Karen's front door, and he enters their house. He is called THE MAN in this play.

THE MAN. I came to tell you, John. Dad sent me a letter. He's leaving all his money to you except a small amount, which you'll be in charge of giving to me in checks, which you'll be responsible for mailing to me. You're the one who knows what he is doing. I don't. I'm not responsible enough. I could never make him understand how hard it's been.

JOHN. Well, he's not sick, is he?

THE MAN. I think so, and yet I'm not sure. I haven't seen him. (*Takes out a gun and shoots John.*)

KAREN (*reaches into the top draw of an end table, takes out a gun, and shoots the man, John's brother*). You can't hurt my husband!

THE MAN. (*Close-up of the man. No blood can be seen. The camera moves to his face. He is on the carpet, and the camera moves to a part of his body that is not injured, for a close-up, but the carpet cannot be seen.*) I'm like any other man.

The End

Curtain, if this is a play; a fade-out, if this is a film.

Nights Thinking of Paris

May 2011

A woman in a lace-lined slip sipping champagne waits by a telephone. The telephone is on a night table. There is a small lamp with a white shade on it, which provides a low light and mysterious shadows leave a slight trace of a romantic air about the room. The camera pans the room. A dressing table with perfume, lipstick on it. The bed has a white bedspread on it, slightly pulled down revealing two pillows laying side by side in white pillowcases. The woman looks disappointed, turns out the light, and the audience can hear her pull the bedspread down and get into bed. It appears that she is waiting for a phone call or a visit, which did not occur.

Ann wakes up early. It is 5:00 a.m. She leaves the hotel; it is still dark. She is walking along the streets, passing large art deco buildings, a video store, and a small grocery store with a few people walking out of it in slightly dirty, over-sized clothes with anxious looks on their faces.

Ann is saddened, stepping over puddles of water on the street, looking up at the dark sky and at the art deco buildings with angels carved onto them over the entrance. The light in the first-floor window.

The rain falls, and a deep, body-shuddering loneliness is felt.

Cut to: Ann is in her own home at the kitchen table speaking to a friend, a woman. They are both around fifty years of age but look ten years younger. They are attractive, and both have brown hair. They are drinking coffee.

ANN. I waited for him and he did not come. He didn't even call. Waited in a hotel room, he booked the room. I was alone. I wonder if things are ever going to change—if life is always going to be a series of strange events in a cold, cruel world.

DEBRA. I know what you mean. Try to contact him today. Find out if something happened.

ANN. I hope he's OK. If he is, I would really like to know why he didn't phone me.

Fade out.

It is evening. Ann is home alone.

Turning on the radio, she turns to a classical music station. They are playing Mendelssohn's Scotch Symphony no. 3 in minor op. 56, A Midsummer Night's Dream.

Ann enters her living room. A Persian rug, red and gold and brown covers the floor. There is a large library against the wall with shelves of the classics: William Shakespeare, *Don Quixote* by Miguel De Cervantes, plays by Henrik Ibsen, poetry by Dylan Thomas, and novels by Ernest Hemingway, the Brontë sisters, art books on the work of van Gogh, Toulouse-Lautrec, and many other great books both fiction and nonfiction.

There is a ceiling lamp, an early twentieth-century light fixture, country style, candle sticks, and a light brown covering, allowing low electric light to pass from it, creating shadows on the walls—the feeling of suspense. There is a fireplace with a fire going and a dark sofa across from it, a small television set, a writing table with an ink stand on it, and a brown armchair.

ANN (*speaks to a relative on the phone*). Hello, yes. I have gone to the bank. It was a surprise that Aunt Rose left such a large amount of money to me. I am not sure why she did it. We were not very close. I suppose it was because everyone else in the family she loved was gone, and I am the only one left. I'm going on a cruise. I've heard they are so much fun. Yes, I will be careful. I will be sure to be careful with who I date. Although I don't think I am at too much of a risk of breaking hearts or having my heart broken, as I cannot seem to keep a man around for more than a day. I waited for Peter to meet me, and he never showed up. He didn't even phone. Yes, I will be careful. Speak to you soon.

Ann hangs up the phone.

The phone rings again. It is Peter on the line.

ANN (*speaks to Peter*). Hello. Peter, where were you? I waited in the hotel room all night, and you never showed. You didn't even call me. A problem at the office? Why didn't you try to call me? I don't know why the hotel manager said my line was busy. I'll be home for a few days. Then I'm going on a cruise. Yes, I'd love to see you tomorrow night at my apartment. I understand. I'm not angry. I understand that you could not reach me and it's fine.

A few nights later, Peter visits Ann. It is nine in the evening. Ann and Peter are sitting in Ann's living room on the brown sofa. Peter is a tall man with brown hair and brown eyes with a piercing expression, sometimes lacking warmth. He is handsome though a bit too sophisticated in his dealings with Ann, which sometimes seem to be businesslike. When asked about this, he explains it as a product of years of pressing responsibilities.

PETER. I would like you to take a trip with me instead of this cruise you're taking alone. I have a wonderful idea. We could go to Paris. France is the place to go. It has cozy, romantic chateaus. It's where beauty is found everywhere. The city has the most enchanting cafes where the poets and painters made the most interesting history in the Impressionist movement. The restaurants have the best food in the world. The mountains in the countryside are as unforgettable as those in Switzerland.

Later that evening, after Peter leaves Ann's apartment, Ann sits on the sofa alone reading the journals of Jean Cocteau. Reading aloud, she reads the journals of Cocteau, the poet, playwright, novelist, and film director.

ANN (*reads aloud, she turns to page 46*). "Between Montmartre, where Max Jacob, Reverdy, and Juan Gris lived and Montparnasse… (*Ann turns to page 13.*) Ahh! the publishing house. (*Ann turns to another page*). "The first illumination about dada came to me in a letter from Tristan containing a map of Europe on which he joined hands with a pointing index finger." (*Turns to page 45.*) "The room of Marcel Proust on Boulevard Hausmann was the first dark room where I witnessed almost every day, to be exact to say, every night, because he lived at night. He was still unknown." (*Ann reads further down on this page.*) "In the evening at the corner window of the hotel I used to see a lamp light, the lamp was Rainer Maria Rilkes. He was Rodin's secretary. (*Ann turns back to page 43.*) "I repeat Picasso has always insulted habits and he insults them until this method itself becomes a habit." "Critics judge work and do not know they are judged by them." "Who gives greatness to France? It is Villon, Rimbaud, Verlaine, Baudelaire. All of them were taken to prison. People wanted to throw them out of France." What is France I ask you?" (*Ann turns to page 226.*) "France is forever struggling against herself. I am amused by people that fear France will become a village, France has always been a village. Everyone is a thinker in France. Even fools think. Everyone is on stage. (*Ann turns to page 236.*) In France there exists a disorder which allows new things and surprises. My development took place in the midst of isms. Cubism, Purism, Orphism, Expressionism, Dadaism, Surrealism." Jean Cocteau was born 1889 and is dead. I will go to Paris with Peter.

A week later, Peter and Ann talk on the telephone.

ANN. Did you hear about it, Peter? A tsunami in Japan followed by volcanoes with a 9.0 magnitude killed thousands, and there are floods in the United States and in other parts of the world. We do not know what will occur. Is this world falling apart?

PETER. It might be a good to wait to take our trip. I would like to see you this week.

ANN. Yes.

PETER. I'll phone you tomorrow. I have to check with my colleagues. Some meetings are planned for this week.

The next evening, Peter and Ann speak by telephone again.

PETER. France said they will start engaging in war against an uprising in Libya. The UN sanctions a No-Fly zone. It seems a trip to France would not be good at this time.

ANN. Yes, I heard about it on the news, though they all seem to lack objective reporting no matter what news station you turn to. Only one or two reliable sources are left. America is considering involvement. It seems rather curious and horrible. As a Jewish woman, I am concerned about the precarious state all these uprisings will leave Israel in. It's very suspicious to me. Concern always seems to be aimed at an objective, monetary in nature.

PETER. Unfortunately, we can do nothing to stop it. Well, we will stay in New York City.

ANN. Good night, Peter. (*Ann hangs up the telephone.*)

Ann goes to her bedroom and gets into bed with a book in hand.

ANN (*falls asleep and dreams*)

Ann is running away from something. She does not know what it is. The city streets are wet. Rain falls lightly and it is cold. Then time moves back into the early 1960s. It is sunny. The streets are cleaner in Brooklyn than presently. Children are laughing, some are singing songs. They make up. The words cannot be understood by Ann. She listens harder and wakes up. (*A book is resting on her that she was reading before she fell asleep.*)

ANN (*begins reading in bed again*). "Norman Rockwell My Adventures as an Illustrator." (*Ann turns to page 34.*) "I sometimes think we paint to fulfill ourselves and our lives, to supply the things we want and don't have."

Fade out.

Fade in.

This scene takes place in a restaurant. Peter and Ann are sitting at a table in a fine restaurant in Manhattan. They are drinking red wine. A bottle is at the table, and they are having a cheese soufflé dish. Hot rolls are shared by both of them. It is late afternoon, and they are having a late lunch. Waiters in white uniforms are serving people. The tables are round and well set apart from one another. White table cloths are on the tables. There is a small bouquet of flowers and a single candle in a candle holder. The candles are lit at some of the tables. The candle is lit at this table.

Peter speaks to Ann at the dinner table.

PETER. Ann, I hope you are enjoying your lunch.

ANN. Yes, it is very good.

PETER. I am falling in love with you, Ann.

ANN. I am surprised, Peter. I didn't think you were that fond of me. I mean, there has been no clear sign of that much feeling. Are you sure you are not just a bit lonely?

PETER. I'm sure of it. You and I are... well, not really able to go on alone easily. We're not that young, but still young enough to enjoy everything with the right partner. You are that person, Ann. I feel delighted with your presence, intoxicated by you. I love your mind, and I am always attracted to you. At the same time, I am so comfortable with you. We could have a love affair for life and a great friendship, too, if you feel the same way.

ANN. Peter, I'm not sure. You missed dates with me. I thought you weren't really interested in me. This is happening quickly. I don't know what I feel yet. I think we should see each other for at least a few months before we discuss it again.

PETER. I understand. Well, we shall wait to discuss it again. Could we go back to your apartment for a while to talk and relax? I would like to be alone with you for a while before I go home and prepare for a busy week without your company.

ANN. Yes, Peter, I would like that.

Peter and Ann return to her apartment. They sit on the sofa. Peter has his arm around her shoulder. Peter takes out a jewelry case with a gold necklace in it and gives it to Ann.

PETER. Ann, I bought you this necklace.

ANN. It's beautiful.

PETER. A heart for a dear heart like you. I thought it was perfect.

Fade out.

Fade in. It is late afternoon in the city. Ann is seen leaving her bank after taking out money. The bank name cannot be seen. The camera shot is of Ann leaving the bank. Only the door closing behind her can be seen.

A man is seen looking at Ann. He follows her, walking less than half a block behind her, She does not notice him. He is a large, strange-looking man with watery-blue eyes, a large mustache, sandy-colored hair, and a strange childlike grin. He follows her, walking less than half a block behind her. She does not notice him.

Ann enters her apartment building. He stands at the corner, staring at her for a minute. She notices him staring at her as she enters the front door of her building. Not knowing who he is, she does not think about it further. The man turns the corner and cannot be seen.

The next day, it is late afternoon. Ann leaves her apartment and walks to a jewelry store. She speaks to a saleswoman behind the counter of gold bracelets and necklaces.

ANN. Hello. I thought perhaps I would consider buying a few gold bracelets, more as an investment. What do you suggest?

SALESWOMAN. I have some very attractive bracelets which are always good to have for the future and are charming for evening wear.

The camera moves to Ann leaving the jewelry store. The same man she saw earlier staring at her as she entered her apartment building. The strange, foolish-looking man with the large mustache is staring at her as she leaves the jewelry store. He walks away quickly and turns down the block looking concerned.

Ann walks into her apartment, goes into the kitchen, pours herself a drink of orange juice, then goes to the living room and turns on the television set to the news station. A reporter is speaking about weather conditions. Ann takes off her coat and places it on the sofa.

NEWS REPORTER (*on television reports*). Violent rain storms moved north Saturday, ripping off roofs, toppling trees, bringing the death toll to twenty-six. Possible tornadoes could move into the Atlantic states. More than one hundred tornadoes were spotted across the region. Five deaths, many casualties, in North Carolina. Mobile homes were destroyed. Two rotating storms and tornadoes in Richmond, Virginia, Washington, and Baltimore. Damaged homes and vehicles in Smithfield, North Carolina, and South Carolina.

ANN. *(Takes the remote control for the television and switches off the TV set.)*

A light rain can be heard outside Ann's window. Ann goes to the window to look outside, and the man that she saw earlier who appeared to be following her at the bank and jewelry store is in front of the apartment building. He then walks across the street and looks up at her window. He walks away when Ann sees him.

Fade out.

Fade in. The next evening, Peter and Ann are in her living room. They speak to each other.

ANN. Peter, I'm terribly frightened. A man is following me. I don't know him. I don't know why he is following me.

PETER. Ann, that's terrible. I'm here for you. I'd like to help you. I'd like to find out why he's following you. Strange, you've never seen him before and don't know who he is. I could stay here with you. This is a very unsafe world. It's falling apart. Nothing is easy to understand. We could find out any number of things about this man, and still there will always be something to worry about. No one can bring back the strength and freedom of the past, the calm, clear, happy, more predictable days. I would like to protect you.

ANN. Perhaps that is a good idea.

PETER. I could live with you for a while here, or you could move in to my house. It would give you a chance to see how you like living with me.

Cut to: The dinner table in Ann's apartment. Peter has moved in to her apartment to be with her. It is evening, a few weeks from the night that he first moved in.

PETER. What's troubling you, Ann?

ANN. I thought we might go out this weekend.

PETER. How about the museum and dinner afterward?

ANN. That sounds very good.

Cut to:

Day inside the Metropolitan Museum of Art. Peter and Ann are looking at some paintings by Paul Cézanne.

ANN. Look, Peter, it is *The Gulf of Marseilles Seen from L'Estaque*, an oil on canvas. It was created in the 1880s. Paul Cézanne painted a dozen of this view—a panoramic view from the town of L'Estaque toward a low range of mountains across the gulf of Marseilles. It is very interesting. I have always loved his relationship to dimension and shape. A sensual French way of seeing heights or shifting his vision to make the wide body of water the main part of the picture so that the mountains and the houses on opposite sides appear to be the same size.

PETER. It is very interesting.

ANN. *The Card Players.* That was a painting by Cézanne that one can never forget. The card players look so real and absorbed in the game. They look like they are concerned about winning and would not tolerate a sound in the room, will get up once the game is over, but never argue, perhaps used to each other's company. He again worked with form so that they are not exactly true to nature in form, but true to nature in the life of man.

PETER. I like the work of Claude Monet as well. Here is a painting I like very much—*La Grenoullère*. It's a swimming spot with a boat rental and a café on the Seine. Renoir and Monet lived near each other in Saint Michel, a few miles from Paris.

Ann and Peter look at the painting by Monet.

The same man that Ann saw following her at the bank, jewelry store, and by her apartment house appears in the museum by the entrance to the room they are looking at the painting in. The man quickly leaves the room once he sees Ann looking at him.

ANN. Peter, that man over there. He is the one I saw following me. Did you see him?

PETER. I don't see a man here. There is no one here but you and me. A woman just passed by, but I don't see a man. Let's go out of the room. Perhaps he left and we can find him.

ANN. Yes, let's do that.

They exit the room and walk along the floor. Some people are looking at paintings and are walking by.

ANN (*looks nervous and frightened*). I don't see him. I'm tired. I feel like going home.

PETER. Yes, I understand. You will feel better once you are home.

Peter puts his arm around Ann, and they exit the floor and walk to the elevator to leave the museum.

Cut to:

This scene opens to Ann in her library. It's a small room in her apartment with a desk and a chair and bookshelves with gold-bound books on it. An armchair and a painting of flowers by an unknown artist is on the wall. Ann removes the painting on the wall and a safe is seen on the wall. Ann turns a combination lock, left three times, right one turn, and left four turns. The safe opens. Ann checks the safe to see if her valuables are inside.

ANN (*speaks to herself*). The money and jewelry are gone. Who could have gotten into the safe? It has not been broken into. No one has the combination. Yet someone had to know it to open the safe.

Peter is sitting on the sofa in the living room, drinking a glass of soda.

ANN. Peter, I don't know how this could have happened. Someone has gotten the combination to my safe.

PETER. I didn't know you had a safe.

ANN. All my money and jewelry are gone.

PETER. I hope you didn't keep everything in it.

ANN. Of course not. I have a bank account. I kept over fifty thousand in the safe.

PETER. That much money?

ANN. Yes, and a couple of gold bracelets, rings, and watches.

PETER. Ann, I'm so sorry. Who do you think it was?

ANN. That man that was following me. I don't know who he is. He's been following me for weeks to the bank and jewelry store. That must be it. He's found out where I keep my money and what I buy. But I don't know how he found out about the safe.

PETER (*said in a puzzled voice*). Are you sure you don't know who he is?

ANN. I've never seen him before a few weeks ago. I couldn't help noticing that he was following me. Everywhere I went, I saw him. That's funny, if he was following me, why does he make it so obvious?

PETER. That is curious. Are you sure you didn't write down the combination and then lose it?

ANN. No, I never took the number out of the house. How could he have found it if I never took it out of the house?

PETER. Ann, I hope you don't think I would ever hurt you. I would like you to trust me completely. I want to marry you. I've fallen in love with you.

ANN. Of course, I don't think anything of the kind. You've been supportive through this very frightening time—this odd time. It's disappointing to at last have everything I need, never have to work in an office again, and then made miserable by this man following me everywhere. I had a hard time all my life—struggling, never making enough money, saving on everything, not being able to achieve my goals, finding myself, no time to really find out if I had what it takes to be an artist that could make money, no chance to improve on my work as a painter, and no connections to or time to find a gallery interested in my work. I never went on a vacation long enough to leave the country. Then my aunt died and left me a fortune. I wanted to spend all my time on my art and to see the wonderful places in the world I never could get away to see before.

Fade out.

Fade in. It is evening on the same night. The scene takes place in a city street in front of a grocery store. Peter and the man Ann saw following her are talking to each other.

PETER. I don't know if we could accomplish anything further, unless I could get her to marry me. I got everything in the safe. She keeps the rest of her money in a bank. The money that is worth going after.

FRANK. If you can't get her to marry you, what are you going to do?

PETER. I don't know. I see no reason to harass her. It would be a lot of work to find someone to forge her signature and to work on looking exactly like her.

FRANK. I could follow her more often while you console her and wine and dine her.

Peter and Frank can be seen talking, but the audience can no longer hear them as the camera moves to a close-up shot of Ann approaching the candy store. She catches the last part of what Peter and Frank have been saying to each other.

ANN (*speaks to herself*). I have been deceived. Peter is trying to rob me. He may try to hurt me or kill me. I'm so alone. Nothing gets better for me. I thought he was my friend and a man that was beginning to love me and cared about me enough to have only my interest at heart. How could I have been so deceived? (*Ann begins to cry softly.*)

Ann exits the street corner. Walking quickly, she turns down another street.

Ann enters a diner to have a cup of coffee and contemplate what to do about Peter. She sits at a table, and a waitress approaches her.

The waitress is an elderly woman with a businesslike approach to waitressing. Her voice is without warmth and she speaks in a direct manner.

WAITRESS (*approaches Ann, speaks to her*). Would you like a menu?

ANN. Yes, thank you.

WAITRESS (*hands Ann the menu*). I'll be back in a few minutes to take your order.

ANN (*studies the menu*). Thank you.

A man enters the diner. He recognizes Ann, having worked with her previously in a lawyer's office. His name is James.

JAMES (*goes to Ann's table and speaks to her*). Ann, hello. I was hoping to see you again.

ANN. James, I thought you moved to California.

JAMES. No. I decided to stay here. I've got my own agency now.

ANN. Your own detective agency?

JAMES. That's right. Two men work with me. One helps in research and investigates the person I need information on, and the other assists the researcher and helps me when needed. I take the cases I want to take now.

ANN. I have a problem—a very bad problem.

JAMES. I'm sorry to hear that. I would very much like to help you. I always liked you, Ann. I was breaking up with Evelyn when we met.

ANN. I understand. I hope everything is all right now.

JAMES. Yes, very much so. What can I do for you? Do you need my services?

ANN. I do. I met a man at the time my Aunt Rose passed away. She left me a fortune, very unexpected. We weren't close, but no one was left to leave it to. He's been telling me he loves me. He wants to marry me. I found it hard to believe. At first, he missed a few dates. I should reveal to you, he even missed a meeting with me in a hotel room he booked. Then a strange man began following me. A somewhat heavyset man, foolish-looking, with a foolish, menacing grin and a large mustache—like something men might have had in the nineteenth century, a handlebar mustache—and watery blue eyes. I saw him outside my apartment building, the bank, and at the jewelry store I shopped at. Staring at me, he always tried to make eye contact with me. Then he'd smile stupidly and quickly walk away. Peter and I went to the museum, and I saw him there too. I left, and when I came home, I entered my library—a small room where I keep a desk and some classics and a painting that covers a wall safe. I opened the safe, and fifty thousand dollars, jewelry, a few bracelets, and watches worth at least ten thousand dollars were gone. I spoke to Peter, but he said he couldn't imagine how it could have happened, unless I lost the combination and perhaps the man following me found it. He said I might have taken the paper I had the combination written on out of the house. I never took it out, and when I looked for it, it was where I keep it in my desk draw. I left the apartment for a walk and saw Peter outside a small grocery store, a small store that sells candy and groceries. He was talking to the man that had been following me. Peter said that he got all the money and jewelry out of the safe, and everything else I had was in the bank. That he would have to marry me to get that, and then the man promised him he would increase the times he followed me until Peter figured out what to do.

Waitress appears at the table Ann is sitting at with James.

WAITRESS. You have a friend that has joined you. Shall I get you a menu, sir?

JAMES. Can I join you for lunch, Ann?

ANN. Of course.

JAMES (*to waitress*). I'll see a menu, thank you.

ANN (*to waitress*). I'll wait to order until my friend does.

WAITRESS. I'll be back in a few minutes.

JAMES. I'll buy lunch, Ann.

ANN. How kind of you.

WAITRESS (returns and waits for orders)

ANN. I'll have a salad, Italian dressing, and coffee.

JAMES. That's all?

ANN. Yes.

JAMES. I'll have the same.

JAMES (*to Ann*). I'm sorry you are going through so much. So Peter is working with that creep to rob you of everything you have.

ANN. Yes. I thought it would be so much better now. I was sorry that my aunt passed on. She was an elderly woman. I never got along well with her at any time in our lives. I thought now that she left me so much money, everything was going to be perfect. I would have fun, live well, and have no problems.

JAMES. Think hard. Have you ever seen the man that is following you at any time in the past?

ANN. No, I haven't.

JAMES. It sounds like he's experienced in harassing people. And as far as Peter is concerned, he could have set up other women, possibly marrying some, then taken their money or even murdered some of his victims. Very convincing, wasn't he?

ANN. Yes, I doubted him only once, but he had a way of bringing the conversation around to my problems before I could ask him any questions about his motives.

JAMES. I'll take care of it, Ann. I want to know everything you know about Peter. If you know where he works, where he lives, and if he has family that you know of and friends.

ANN. I know very little about him. He speaks about the enormous work he has and meetings he must attend. But I do not know where he works.

JAMES. The first thing you must do is to change the locks on your door. I will go home with you tonight to make sure Peter, if he is already there, is forced to leave. An all-night locksmith I know can change the lock as soon as we get him out. I will work on recovering your money and jewelry. Check his background, see if he got caught committing other crimes, follow him to see what he's up to. Once I know, we can at least keep him from finding further interest in you. I hope to do more, but that's a start.

ANN. Thank you.

JAMES. I usually get one hundred dollars a day, but since we know each other and I like you, Ann, I'll take half of that to cover expenses and pay a few bills. Is that okay?

ANN. Yes, that's great.

Waitress approaches.

WAITRESS (*speaks to Ann and James*). Can I bring you anything else?

ANN. No, thank you.

JAMES (*to the waitress*). I'll take the check.

ANN (*to James*). I'm glad I met you.

Scene ends.

This scene takes place in Ann's apartment. It is ten o'clock in the evening. Peter is watching television, sitting on Ann's sofa alone. Ann and James enter the apartment.

ANN. Peter, I would like you to pack your things quickly and leave my apartment.

PETER. What are you saying, Ann?

ANN. I won't go into it. I don't want to see you here again. I never want to see you again.

JAMES. I am here to protect Ann. I don't know what else you have done, but I know what you've done to her. After you leave here tonight, I'm going to find out more about you. I can let you know that because you will never see me following you, and there are many ways to look into your past. My colleagues and I will be working on it. I am working for Ann. You will return the money and jewelry you took from the safe. I expect you to contact me to do that. Ann saw you talking to that man you hired to harass her. It seems he had experience in that line of work. I'll be here tonight while you pack. In fact, I'll be here all night.

PETER. I'll pack right now and be out in less than an hour.

ANN. I expect you to contact James to return my money and jewelry.

PETER. I will have it by tomorrow. You're not going to the police, are you?

JAMES. I'm a private detective working for Ann. My decisions have to do with her welfare, so you'll help me to decide what to do.

PETER. I'll be out of the country after I give you the money and jewelry.

JAMES. That will make it easier for you since there's no telling what I may find out about you. I'm a private detective. I don't work for the government. My direction, my motives, and my morals are never divided. I work for the individual—a cleaner occupation, especially these days. But I can't obstruct what they call justice. If you're not in this country after you return her money and jewelry—well, it might be to your advantage.

PETER. I'll pack right now.

Cut to a few days later. Ann is in James's office. His desk is large and neat; a filing cabinet is behind him. A small computer and a telephone is on the desk.

JAMES (*to Ann*). I found out a few things about Peter and the man he had following you. Peter has never been convicted of a crime. He was married to a woman who mysteriously died. They found her in a lake in upstate New York. It was considered a suicide. They separated at the time, and her family—a sister and a brother—remembered her being very depressed. Peter was living in New York City. She was living in the Catskills. She cut him off when they separated. She was wealthy. There was nothing unusual before that. No disappearance of money or jewels. She put all her money into houses which are now owned by her family and accounts they now have in their names. I mentioned to you that I am a private detective, and this is the reason. The man Peter had following you works for the federal government. He has a job to harass people and anyone that the government would like to make miserable. Unfortunately, this is now considered surveillance. He is one of the many people the government has made a deal with. He previously worked for loan sharks, harassing people. His immediate family is connected and now disconnected to crime figures that are in prison. The creep had a job with the State to cover his criminal activity. I am confused about what it was. Pumping gas for an agency, I believe. Recently, ten bodies were found at his previous job site. They were found buried there, and an investigation is underway. This is also in the upstate region, though I doubt they will connect him to it even if he is involved. He is one of the richest men in the upstate region. We can see how he made most of his money. He was working for Peter to harass you. The hope was that you would become so frightened of his constant presence that you would marry Peter.

ANN. Will I continue to be harassed?

JAMES. No, because even if I may not be able to do anything about Frank since he works for the federal government, Peter is frightened that I may get something on him, and I will. But again, owing to the changes in the country and the denial of justice to people who often deserve it more than the people that so often get it, it is better that he remains frightened and leaves the country. His decision to do that tells me he won't bother you again. If he does leave, I will know it. I will be following him after I get your money and jewels. I'll be back to tell you about it. I will see him tomorrow night to do that.

ANN. Thank you so much. I don't know what I would have done if I didn't have your help.

JAMES. I will see to it that you are completely free of this monster and his accomplice before I close this case. I will also have more on these men in my files to use as needed. When the right time to move on it comes up, I'll be ready if we need to.

This scene takes place in Paris, France. Peter is with an American woman. They are seated at a table, which is placed outside. The café has tables inside and outside of it. And they have finished a cup of coffee.

PETER. I've had such a wonderful time since I met you. Let's go back to my hotel suite tonight, Alice.

ALICE. That's a great idea.

Cut to: Peter's hotel suite in Paris, which is large and comfortable. There is a small dining area, two chairs, and a table. They are seated at the table. It is still evening, and Alice and Peter are having another cup of coffee.

Peter suddenly chokes, falls from his seat, becomes ill, and is dying. He has been poisoned.

PETER (*speaks to Alice*). What is happening?

ALICE. I am Carey's sister. Your ex-wife, you remember. You murdered her and made it look like suicide with that man that was harassing her. We have a large family. We were waiting for a chance to pay you back for the misery and horror you put her through. You won't take apart more wonderful and loving people. I'll be leaving now. No one will find out what it is that killed you. What I put in your coffee leaves no trace.

The End

TREATMENT FOR THE MAN ON THE STREET IS WITHOUT A PRAYER

The Man on the Street Is Without a Prayer is the speech of our time and a hilarious comedy. It is the classic screenplay of our time that will create a wave of art and invite a new generation of film buffs that presently need the work of Woody Allen, John Cleese, and the love to see the Marx brothers.

The characters are unforgettable and symbolic of life in the twenty-first century. Jacob Paul Buddaman, the hero of our story, is released from the Downgrade Hospital for the Sick and the Depressed. He leaves his friends behind, fellow patients at the hospital: Tina, an angry pregnant woman who plans to place a bomb in her boyfriend's beeper; four men who believe they are apostles to God, which they believe Jacob Paul Buddaman to be; two new patients; and a man who thinks he is a lamb and a sumo wrestler that would like to be called a pseudo wrestler and is health conscious.

The pseudo wrestler flings a sadistic aide in the air as the aide tries to take his rickshaw away. The pseudo wrestler uses the rickshaw to carry cans of string beans in to eat, prior to a match with his opponent.

Jacob Paul Buddaman is discharged from the Downgrade Hospital for the Sick and the Depressed by Dr. Mannose. Dr. Mannose falls into sucking his thumb during sessions with patients and flying into tantrums about his life as a psychiatrist once alone in his office. Jacob Paul Buddaman leaves the hospital and attempts to stay with his friend Nero. Nero's wife objects to it. Jacob tries to convince her that he is a good influence since he has stopped Nero from setting fires in Queens, New York, and eating clay and banishing her from the house.

Fortunately, Jacob meets an old high school friend, Benny, who lives in an abandoned building; and they survive by begging for food. Jacob, who believed he was God in high school and had followers, now thinks he might be a messenger. He seems to be one, performing heroic feats. He is a philosopher, strange and wonderful.

After eating a spoiled piece of chicken given to him by the angry manager of the Chicken Right restaurant, he has a hallucination and sees four commandments written on the aspirin tablets that fly out of the aspirin bottle in the drugstore window. The aspirins grow larger and larger, and the commandments are written on the aspirin tablets. Commandment 1: Man, woman, dogs, cats, and bugs were created with a brain and a heart. Everyone has feelings. Man sometimes has feelings too. If your heart hurts, cushion yourself with your arm. If your arm aches, seek refuge in the fly overhead. If the fly does not bring comfort, lie down and dream. If your dream is to build a hill, build it as high as your strength allows. If there is love in your life, build a mountain effortlessly. Commandment 1½ and 2½: Do not steal from the poor to give to yourself. Do not sell your mother-in-law into slavery even if they promise to let her outlive her usefulness. He recites the four commandments and draws a crowd. There is a fade-out here, and we are taken to the year 2093. One hundred years later, Jacob Paul Buddaman is seen as God by some of the followers of the Amen Mena Pause religion. They believe the advances in science can be used ethically. They meet in Washington Square Park in Manhattan on Wednesdays (which they call Hump Day) to discuss better uses for the advances in science.

In 2093, there are mood cushions and orgasmic head devices and thought replica headsets. A young black student, Vincent, who believes in the Amen Mena Pause religion and that Jacob Paul Buddaman is God, reminds us of Jacob since he is godlike, philosophical, and very caring. He must also remind us to keep alive the idea that man can be godlike through the centuries and resemble other men in the way they think and feel. Vincent is a friend to Ruth—a young, middle-aged, funny, frustrated, single Jewish woman—and councils Ruth on her love life. Ruth later discovers that she is in love with a man that would like a species change to a platypus to stay with the mammal in him.

There should be great actors and actresses that will bring the magic needed to make this a classic, with perfect comic timing in the tradition of the greatest era of comic films, well-timed slapstick, no ugly violence, no sex scenes, and no nudity. There is a comic scene that takes place in the year 1993, outside the Downgrade Hospital for the Sick and the Depressed, where a man and a woman are in the bushes outside the hospital. They should not be seen through the bushes since they are making love there and can move the bushes. The hilarious lines said by the actor and actress while Jacob Paul Buddaman passes the bushes on his way to the bus and his response—which is, of course, not to look into the bushes but to wonder if life has changed outside the hospital— is an example of the beauty that we enjoy in Jacob Paul Buddaman. The movie must be a success because the dialogue, concepts, acting, direction, and at least one star that everyone loves seeing in a comedy makes this the movie to see again and again for audiences of every age. The potential for home video is great as well. It's a classic of our time that the family can enjoy seeing together.

This is an easy-to-produce movie. All the scenes take place in Manhattan or on sets that are easy to produce. The Writers Guild stipulates payment for the writer, which I would be very happy to receive, and I would be available to work with other writers (if needed) for the screenplay version. This is written as a screenplay, which allows the director to see what creative changes may be added. I would like to play a small part in this movie.

This letter is intended to interest an agent to represent me, as well as a producer to provide a budget for this screenplay and to bring it to movie theaters—hopefully, around the world. It would be great to attract a director who is also a producer, and I am trying to do this. I work with some of the greatest comic geniuses and artists of our time that are working on getting this screenplay in the right hands. However, I need an agent to represent me when this happens, and so I hope you will contact me if you are the agent to do this. And should a producer that I am sending this treatment to wish to provide a budget, I look forward to receiving a reply by mail as well. I have been reviewed by legends in the arts, and I have some very good reviews, which can be seen on the cover of my book *Robo Sapiens*. Please also see the enclosed business cards in this mailing.

Please contact me at my home address:

Laura Lonshein Ludwig
71 Joel M. Austin Rd. North
Cairo, New York 12413

I live in the countryside in upstate New York. My phone number is 518-622-9747.

I am listed in *Who's Who in the World* as a screenwriter, satirist, and the creator of a top-rated TV show, *Earth Is Not on Tape*, which ran for approximately eleven years, featuring artists and legends in the arts. I was nominated for the Pushcart Prize and am the recipient of four New York State Council on the Arts grants from Poets and Writers. I am the author of four full-length books of screenplays, stage plays, satires, poetry, and a novella, which also makes a good movie. The books are *Robo Sapiens, Sounds Like a Plot, Reflections for the Renaissance, The Haunted House and the Stolen Gold*, and *Gulliver of New York*. Published by Xlibris Corporation, a division of Random House, these are available on all major websites, such as Barnes & Noble Booksellers. My books are listed in the New York Public Library, in libraries around the world, and in good bookstores. I have performed my work on TV and radio for fourteen years and studied acting at the Gene Frankel Theatre. My life as a writer has been inspiring. As I mentioned above, I have outstanding reviews from legends in the arts, great comic actors, and professors who teach at leading universities and drama studies.

I look forward to hearing from you on your interest in this screenplay, *The Man on the Street Is Without a Prayer*—which can be found in two of my books, *Robo Sapiens* and *Reflections for the Renaissance*, on all major websites, libraries, and bookstores around the world.

Sincerely,
Laura Lonshein Ludwig,
Screenplay writer of
The Man on the Street Is Without a Prayer

Listed in Who's Who in the World
Work in the Mid-Manhattan Library and other Libraries

Laura Lonshein Ludwig
Screenplay Writer
To bid for screenplays or with any questions

Write to
71 Joel M. Austin Rd. North
Cairo, NY 12413 Telephone: 518-622-9747

Resident poet of the *Joe Franklin Memory Lane* show, producer for a top-rated TV show for twelve years hosting variety talent and writers, published in over fifty literary magazines, marketing screenplays, actress, director, producer, writer, performer.

Author of books *Robo Sapiens, Sounds Like a Plot, Reflections for the Renaissance, The Haunted House and the Stolen Gold*, and *Gulliver of New York*, and screenplays, novels, stage plays, and poetry sold in good bookstores. The major websites are amazon.com, **www.bn.com**, and **www.xlibris.com**. Phone Xlibris Corporation at 1-888-795-4274.

THE MAN ON THE STREET IS WITHOUT A PRAYER

Laura Lonshein Ludwig © 1992 Writers Guild
Cast of Characters

JACOB PAUL BUDDA-MAN	Male leading role. God and founder of the Amen Mena Pause religion.
MS. RATCHETYWRY	The nurse at the Downgrade Hospital for the Sick and the Depressed.
RALPH	Ms. Ratchetywry's cruel assistant at the hospital.
DAVE	One of the four apostles.
HERALDO	One of the four apostles.
CLARK	One of the four apostles.
KENT	One of the four apostles.
DR. MANNOSE	Hospital psychiatrist.
PSEUDO WRESTLER	Patient at the hospital.
STU LAMB	Patient at the hospital dressed as a lamb.
ESCORT GUARD	Delivers new patients. Hospital guard.
MALE LOVER	Lover in the bushes in front of the hospital.
FEMALE LOVER	Lover in the bushes in front of the hospital.
TINA	The fallen one at the hospital.

BENNY	Old friend of Jacob's.
BRUNO	Skinhead at the Bowery.
MAGGOT	Skinhead at the Bowery.
PAULY	Skinhead at the Bowery.
RALPH	Kind-hearted owner of grocery.
ARNIE BENEDICT	Manager of the Chicken Right Restaurant in the year 1993.
MAN IN THE CROWD	Observes Jacob speaking in the street.
SECOND MAN IN THE CROWD	Observes Jacob speaking in the street.
OLDER WOMAN IN THE CROWD	Observes Jacob speaking in the street.
TEENAGE GIRL IN THE CROWD	Listens to Jacob speaking in the crowd.
MAN PASSING JACOB	Man with woman who passes Jacob as he lies in the street.
WOMAN PASSING JA-COB	Woman with man passes Jacob as he lies in the street.
PEDRO	Construction worker in the year 2093.
JUNIOR	Construction worker in the year 2093.
RICHARD	Construction worker in the year 2093.
KEVIN	Construction worker in the year 2093.
BOY	Young boy in dysfunctional family.
GIRL	Young girl in dysfunctional family.

MOTHER	Mother to boy and girl in dysfunctional family in the year 2093.
VINCENT	Male student of life who follows the Amen Mena Pause religion in the year 2093.
DELORES	Female college student admired by Vincent in the year 2093.
RUTH SHLEPER	Actress looking for that special someone in the year 2093.
ARNIE BARNACLE	Manager of the Chicken Right restaurant in the year 2093.
HOMELESS MAN OF THE FUTURE	Man seeking food at Chicken Right in the year 2093.
BOY NAMED SUE	Teenage boy who robs Arnie Barnacle at the Chicken Right Restaurant in the year 2093.
PETER	Telemarketer at the Squarebud Theatre in the year 2093.
RHONDA INKWELL	Manager at the Squarebud Theatre in the year 2093.
JIM	Telemarketer at the Squarebud Theatre who is living in a world of his own and is the heart's desire of Ruth Shleper in the year 2093.
HAROLD HARVEED III	Financial director of the Squarebud Theatre in the year 2093.
THEODORE WINCE	Snob of the future. Assistant to Howard Harveed III at the Squarebud Theatre in the year 2093.
ROGER WRIGHT	Snob of the future. Assistant to Howard Harveed III at the Squarebud Theatre in the year 2093.

MARJORIE LONG	Assistant to Howard Harveed III at the Squarebud Theatre in the year 2093. A snob climbing the walls of advancement.
MARSHA HARBOR	Verbal snob alongside her colleagues at the Squarebud Theatre in the year 2093. Assistant to Howard Harveed III.
MARY SCOTT II	Assistant to the Howard Harveed III at the Squarebud Theatre. Appears to be somehow related to royalty. Works in the Squarebud Theatre in the year 2093.

FADE IN.

INT. PSYCHIATRIC WARD - DOWNGRADE HOSPITAL FOR THE SICK AND DEPRESSED (BROOKLYN) - EARLY EVENING

JACOB PAUL BUDDAMAN, the star of this story, is standing in the middle of the dayroom surrounded by FOUR MEN. He wears a sheet thrown over his body, which looks like a Roman toga. His head is shaven and he has one earring in one ear. In the other ear, he also wears an earring, which he is putting on as he speaks to the four men. One earring is a Jewish star, the other a cross from the Christian religion. His robe has three pins on it. One pin says, "Men may control the world, but can they fake orgasms?" One button reads, "I do the work of three men: Moe, Larry, and Curly." One button, which holds the sheet in place at the center of his chest, reads, "Man belongs to this earth, earth does not belong to man."

The four men surrounding him also wear sheets. They believe Jacob is God––or something close to that––and listen to him speak with great reverence. He is the answer to their prayers. He is kind and wise. And even when he is not making complete sense, he seems to be making sense anyway. These four men call themselves the apostles. They call each other, excluding Jacob, "great carriers of thought." They never use birth names when speaking to one another.

Sitting beside them is a YOUNG WOMAN of twenty-six or so. She listens attentively to Jacob's philosophies but does not speak just yet. She is six months pregnant, wears a T-shirt that reads "Baby on Board," and is as tough as a bed of nails. She speaks in response to MS. RATCHETYWRY, the nurse who calls all the patients for medication. When her name, TINA, is called, she reminds the nurse that she wants to be known as the fallen one.

Jacob is speaking to the APOSTLES; he speaks slowly and deliberately, although he is often distracted by the medication nurse, Ms. Ratchetywry, who nods her head in approval as he speaks, then is eyed inquisitively by Jacob, and she then turns her head away, pretending not to listen.

Ms. Ratchetywry is in her early forties and overweight. She is very nice, but in her effort to compensate for the life she and her patients must live, and for RALPH, her cruel assistant, she is often too nice. She is limited at the same time in her ability to perceive all the components of any one situation.

Ms. Ratchetywry stands over the medication tray in an anxious state of mind and calls each patient to come up for medication in a slow and clear voice. She wears a pin on her dress (not a uniform) that has her name on it. At the far end of the room, opposite to the side of Ms. Ratchetywry, is her assistant, Ralph. He is seated, is thin, mean as a snake, wears a ring in his nose, is Caucasian, and has a tattoo on his arm that reads, "I'm your backdoor man." He always has a straightjacket in his hands when sitting down. He fondles the straightjacket at these times.

JACOB

And you see, my young apostles, there is no way out. We must not fall for that easy answer. Gonna marry my woman, gonna rape the land, gonna rape my woman, and get as fat as I can. You see, that rhymed, but then you could do that too. You must see what I am saying. We must save ourselves from becoming high-minded swine. You know, a couple of centuries from now, there will be religious art again, and where would we be? Flat art with a picture of me in the middle of it—that's not what I want. We are not here to suffer and die because we are allowing the animal in us...

MS. RATCHETYWRY

Tina, Jacob, Paul, and the apostles I mean Dave, Clark, come. It is medication time.

TINA

Ms. Ratchetywry, don't call me Tina anymore. That was my old name. I'm the Fallen One, got it? The Fallen One. Now, do you see how pregnant I am? Well, so does everyone else. But that don't matter anymore, because every dog had his day and if I get out of this hole alive, I'm going to kill Pedro with his own beeper. I will. I will put a bomb in that beeper and blow his head off. Do you know this is the fourth time he's knocked me up, and every single time he says he wears a rubber. I don't know, because when I'm hot, I'm not thinking about that. But anyway, these other girls call him on that beeper I gave him, and I know it. That was my present to him for the biggest drug sale he ever made, and that made me proud, you know? But this screwing around is going to be—

MS. RATCHETYWRY

(nodding, looking at Tina as she continues to call names)
The Fallen One, the apostles, and Jacob Buddaman, this is your last call. I have to move on now to other things.

Ralph holds his straightjacket firmly in his hands and begins to sensually touch its fabric. He looks at the patients sadistically.

Jacob and the apostles answer together as they look at Ralph.

JACOB AND APOSTLES
(angelically)
Coming right away, Ms. Ratchetywry.

JACOB

Ahh, the juice is good for you and so good too. It has the same delicious flavor, and yet so hard to find, that my little cactus had. Ahh, my cactus... so easy to maintain, and with water, it's delicious for dinner in those more conservative years when the cactus juice wasn't trickling down fast enough from the great wealth of our nation.

These small pills are not so good though. They put me to sleep, and I have so much to think about.

The apostles are really named Dave, Clark, Kent, and Heraldo.

APOSTLES
(together)

Yes, I think you have something there.

TINA

Why do I have to take this medicine, Ms. Ratchetywry? It's not going to stop me from killing Pedro. Maybe I'll just turn him in to the police one night when he's working a full load, then I'll come to prison to visit him and tell him I'm in love with his best friend, Dukey. Now, Ms. Ratchetywry, does that sound better?

MS. RATCHETYWRY

Well, I'm glad to hear you've changed your ways, because Dr. Mannose is making his rounds tonight, and if he hears you talking about violence, he might stick you in the junior ward. Lock up violent thinkers, where there's no television past eight, and so you'd miss your favorite show, *Murder She Wrote*.

Medication is given to the patients. After medication, Tina is in a chair not far from Ms. Ratchetywry, sitting in a thinking position, looking, oddly enough, very intellectual.

Ms. Ratchetywry is dusting the counter where she sits. Jacob and the apostles are sitting together, looking very saintly. Ralph, the sadistic assistant to Ms. Ratchetywry, has fallen asleep in his chair. His face lifts and drops periodically as he sleeps. He looks like an old man who is hardened, but in a rest state.

A large white clock is high on the wall and reads 7:00 p.m. Everyone rushes to the television set, which is in the center of the room they are in. It is an old television; a model from the early 1960s. The room is stark, except for some drawings on the wall and some chairs.

Ms. Ratchetywry notices it is 7:00 p.m. and leaves the counter area to sit in a chair and watch television with the patients. Everyone else grabs a chair or moves their chair to get close to the television. From the television, they hear a flash sound.

Everyone in the room, including Ms. Ratchetywry—except for Ralph, who is asleep–speaks at once, in time with the television announcer. The show and the announcer are not visible; only the announcer can be heard, saying:

> ANNOUNCER (O/C)
> "Welcome to *Jeopardy* with Alex Trebek."

> JACOB
> Tools that begin with the letter *R*. Uh, uh... one of many rotating finishing tools with spiral or straight fluted cutting edges for finishing a hole to size and shape... uh-huh, let me see... tools that begin with uh, let me see... it's kind of like a swirling thing. It goes up—way up, and plunges through all the defiance to the core. It... it's used to cut the edge of a soft, pliable, warm...
> (dreamily)
> butt... I mean um, wood... it's a reamer.

> TINA
> *R*, huh? I ain't about to tell ya how smart I am. I'll let you guess. A book moth I'm not. I may be a diamond in the rougher place, but I could make mountains out of moles' hills. A coarse form of file, having separate point-like teet...h sounds like my mother, but it's not... a person grating, grating... on your nerves like a file, I think ...oh yeah, when I built my loft... a rasp.

(excited and happy)

Oh, oh my god, I'm sorry, Jacob. I didn't mean to use your name in vain. I got the answer.

Everyone hugs Tina, and Jacob hugs the apostles. Ralph snorts in his sleep.

MS. RATCHETYWRY

(giggling)

Now it's my turn. *R...* tools. What kind of tool turns something... turns and turns but causes it to move in only one direction? Twists and turns... Oh my, I have it on the tip of my tongue. I can just taste it. Riffler! No, that's completely wrong, that's a potato chip. Router is something I've heard of... Wait a minute...

(looking at everyone in disbelief but pridefully)

Could it be a ratchet? Oh my god, I'm right! Right as rain.

Everyone applauds and Ralph wakes up, looking mean and rubbing his eyes like a boy.

At this point, the lights lower or the scene is changed.

FADE OUT.

FADE IN.

INT. PSYCHIATRIC WARD - DOWNGRADE HOSPITAL FOR THE SICK AND DEPRESSED (BROOKLYN) - NEXT DAY - MIDAFTERNOON

The apostles are playing checkers. Tina is reading a magazine. Ms. Ratchetywry approaches Jacob.

MS. RATCHETYWRY

(placing her hand on Jacob's shoulder)

Jacob, how are we doing today?

JACOB

Oh, Ms. Ratchetywry, you needn't stand on ceremonies with me. I know something is troubling you, or you'd stop asking me if I'm doing well.

MS. RATCHETYWRY
(quickly removing her hand from Jacob's shoulder in a puzzled state)
Yes, Jacob. You're always so right. Now...
(lift her eyes to the air, as if in prayer)
Jacob, Dr. Mannose would like to see you. I believe it's about your leaving us. So go right through that door and he will discuss your discharge plans.

Ralph is sitting near the doorway that Jacob will enter. He is looking Jacob up and down as if he is a good person to put in a straightjacket and is getting away.

INT. DR. MANNOSE'S OFFICE

DR. MANNOSE is sitting in a large leather chair. The room Jacob enters is small. Dr. Mannose has papers in a heap on his desk. He looks like Einstein; his hair is to his shoulders but is cut to look like Einstein. He is wearing a black tie and vest and a long-sleeved white shirt. He is sucking his thumb as Jacob enters. He quickly takes his thumb out of his mouth as Jacob's eyes meet his.

DR. MANNOSE

Come in, Jacob.

JACOB

Yes, Dr. Mannose, thank you. What a lovely office you have.

DR. MANNOSE

Be seated, Jacob. Good. Now don't be shy, tell me the truth. How are we doing?

JACOB

That's funny, I didn't think you were doing so bad, being a doctor and all... but really, Dr. Mannose, I don't know you, as

well as Ms. Ratchetywry and I, don't know how you're doing.
I'm doing very well, though.

DR. MANNOSE

No, Jacob, I'm doing just fine, and I'm glad you asked because
that shows you're thinking clearly. I think you've made some
great strides in your drugging here.
(putting his thumb in his mouth)
I mean your stay here. But I want to hear it from you. Is it true
that you've realized that you're not God anymore?

JACOB

I believe that we all have a mission in life.

DR. MANNOSE

Yes, Jacob, and what is your mission in life?

JACOB

To make myself productive, perhaps as a messenger now.

DR. MANNOSE

Oh, you will start with a simpler job, like a messenger. Easier
than carrying mail, I suppose.

JACOB

Yes. It is easier than working with those lunatics. Yes, it may
not be much in the eyes of those who are in the habit of
manipulating others for money or for beliefs they themselves
find hard to really believe in.

DR. MANNOSE becomes very uncomfortable, wriggles around
in his chair, and puts his thumb in his mouth for a moment, then
withdraws it quickly.

DR. MANNOSE

What do you mean by that, Jacob?

JACOB

I mean, Doctor, there are finer things out there than fitting in
and buying a house with a garage and marrying a wife that must
have a new house, even if our jobs won't pay for it. Actually,

if you're going to marry, always look for a woman who loves life instead––a woman who loves nature and good books and me for me. But marriage is not in my plans for now. For now, I must work as a messenger and volunteer my time to the sick and the aged, the poor and the poorer, and to every individual that has been affected by the modern day McCarthyism of our generation.

Jacob is self-absorbed but notices Dr. Mannose lightly dropping off to sleep. As Jacob completes his thought, he wakes with a start, becoming insecure. Once again, he puts his thumb in his mouth.

> DR. MANNOSE
>
> I,... I see. Well, and uh, how do you feel about that?
>
> JACOB
>
> Dr. Mannose, may I ask you a question? Dr. Mannose?
>
> DR. MANNOSE
>
> Well, if it doesn't take too long. There's only five minutes left to our session, and we have to determine whether we can let you out into... the I mean, we must see if it is time to try out some of these new plans in the world.
>
> JACOB
>
> Dr. Mannose, have you always sucked your thumb? Because it doesn't help in our search for truth––our search together––if I see that you are in conflict.
>
> DR. MANNOSE
>
> I... beg your pardon? I think that will be all for today. You can leave us at 4:00 p.m. today. I think you are ready for the world. See Ms. Ratchetywry on the way out for your things. Good luck, Jacob.
>
> JACOB
>
> Thank you, Dr. Mannose. You really are very nice to let me go into the world. My visit with you is useful in my teachings.

DR. MANNOSE
Yes, yes. Well, so long.

Jacob closes the door behind him.

DR. MANNOSE
I always get the lunatics. Why didn't I become a surgeon like my father? I'd rather cut them open than have to listen to them. All day, yak yak yak, "I think I'm God" "I want to diet"––and she's seventy-five pounds… "I'm afraid of this and that." They all change with medicine. At least they shut up with a few thousand bolts of Thorazine in'em. Talk, talk––what does it do? I don't know anymore. My father was a bastard, but I came out okay.

An ESCORT brings patients to Ralph, who is silently sitting by the front door.

CUT TO::

INT. DAY ROOM - DOWNGRADE HOSPITAL FOR THE SICK AND DEPRESSED (BROOKLYN) - LATE AFTERNOON

Jacob enters the dayroom and is seen waiting for Ms. Ratchetywry by the front desk. He is surprised to see through the front door that an escort is bringing Ralph two new patients: a PSEUDO WRESTLER and a MAN dressed as a lamb.

Ralph stands uneasily next to the pseudo wrestler and with the man dressed as a lamb, who is named STU LAMB.

The sumo wrestler holds a rickshaw with canned string beans in it. He is holding in his free hand a psychology book. His real name is Jack, but he likes to be known as the pseudo wrestler, not as a sumo wrestler.

The apostles enter together from the side.

APOSTLES
What do we have here? They really look like they could use some…

APOSTLE NO. 1/DAVE
(great carrier of thought)

Oh my, he thinks he's a lamb. What a sad fate. He calls himself Stu Lamb, I imagine.

APOSTLE NO. 2/ HERALDO

In reply to that, my dear carrier of thought, we do not know ourselves if he is not a lamb. For reality is not understood as well as we would like it to be. Perhaps he is a lamb––for now.

APOSTLE NO. 3/CLARK

Let us ask the great one before he is discharged, and we will be stuck... I mean, we will not know how to help the sumo wrestler and the lamb. Frankly, I will not rely on the hospital to care for me in any emergencies.

APOSTLE NO. 4/KENT

Do not worry. I don't think a fractured hip or a broken jaw will be painful if we don't hit back.

TINA
(enters)

What a hunk... that's a man over there!
(to the apostles, staring at the pseudo wrestler)

I would let him do me any time!

The apostles look at Tina and bow their heads with understanding.

CU on Ralph trying to ask pseudo wrestler for his rickshaw.

RALPH

Welcome to our happy home. Let me take your, um, your rickshaw. I'll store it in a safe place where no one will sell it for what they could get. I mean, it will be safe and protected from thieves... as a person who enters a rest home—I mean a place to rest—should expect and at least deserves, in their needy um, hours.

PSEUDO WRESTLER

I don't need a rest. Someone told me there was a match here and that I could beat my opponent by squashing him like a bug. Where is the match?

RALPH

A match? A match *here*? Who said that?

PSEUDO WRESTLER

I think it was my mother. She's my manager.

RALPH

Well, I am so pleased to meet a sumo wrestler. What is your name—if you'd like to tell me, I mean, what your name is... Your um…

PSEUDO WRESTLER

I am not a sumo wrestler. I am a *pseudo* wrestler. I have come to realize that I have a long way to go before I am centered enough to be sumo. I am finding myself through meditation, better living, less red meat—unless, of course, you count the men I throw around and pulverize. They *want* to be hurt, you know what I mean?

RALPH

(smiles sheepishly)

Ya... yes, I do. Well, that's um, true, and you are a very strong man. And of all the people here, I like you the best. But while you're here, it is my job to get your belongings and keep them safe. Now, may I have your rickshaw, please? It would be very uh, nice, of you, I mean.

(whining like a little boy)

Please?

PSEUDO WRESTLER

What do you mean here? And where do I fight?

Ms. Ratchetywry walks to Stu Lamb and takes his hand and brings him to her desk. She speaks to Ralph as she passes by.

MS. RATCHETYWRY

Ralph, will you put his um, um... Now let me see, they had it on *Jeopardy* the other day.

RALPH

His rickshaw—you mean his rickshaw. Put it away. Ms. Ratchetywry, I hear someone calling me... maybe one of the patients needs help. Ms. Ratchetywry, please don't walk away, because you could take the rickshaw, and I could...

MS. RATCHETYWRY

(matter-of-factly)

Oh, Ralph, no one's calling you. No one calls you. I've been here for twenty years, and your name has never been called by a patient. Now don't be a baby, just take it. He won't hurt you. Besides, we have other things to do. Jacob's leaving us today.

All the patients, in unison, move closer to Ralph and the pseudo wrestler. Ralph lowers his head as he takes a step closer to pseudo wrestler.

RALPH

(whispering and whining a little)

My manhood is at stake here. Would you *please* give me the rickshaw. Please?

PSEUDO WRESTLER

Oh, so this is the opening act. American wrestling is always so corny—hams... Well, if theater is what you want—bad theater—I'll give it to you. Ready, Ralph, for the ride of your life? I'm glad you're puny, because I'm going to pulverize you. You're going to wish you were a baker instead.

(lowering his voice)

I know you don't deserve this, but it's business, you know. Strange audience... looks a little biblical to me.

Jacob and the apostles have a curious but saintly expression on their faces. Tina looks angelic and the Stu Lamb is sitting beside the apostles. Everyone is watching the pseudo wrestler and Ralph.

PSEUDO WRESTLER

And now, for the airplane ride of your life.

Pseudo wrestler picks Ralph up and spins him above his head, spinning him slowly to the right and then to the left. As pseudo wrestler picks up speed, Ralph is being spun more quickly.

RALPH

Oh god, mother of Jesus... I don't deserve this... Help, will someone help me! Eelpppppppppppp!

Everyone breaks into slight smiles as they watch pseudo wrestler spinning Ralph.

MS. RATCHETYWRY

Now, now. We mustn't do this, Mr. um We don't wrestle here. Put the nice man down, and we'll talk about it. Now, now... stop this at once or I will have to call the emergency staff.

PSEUDO WRESTLER

This staff, are they part of the act? I'm not wrestling more than one guy.

He is spinning Ralph more slowly now.

RALPH

For God's sake, put me down! I've been working here for twenty years. Please, put me down!

PSEUDO WRESTLER

You have a good act, Ralph. That's my cue to put you down, right?

RALPH

Yeah, yeah, that's right.

MS. RATCHETYWRY

Please, would you put him down? He'll get sick.

RALPH

I'm sick *now*.

PSEUDO WRESTLER
Lady, I want you to know, whoever you are, that you're great.
You can join my act any time. How much you making now?
Don't want to say, huh? Okay, I understand. Here goes.

Pseudo wrestler drops Ralph to the ground hard after one final
heavy spin around.

Ralph groans and crawls away.

Ms. Ratchetywry takes pseudo wrestler gently by the hand to the back
and out of the room (OC).

The apostles shake their heads in disapproval.

TINA
(obviously stimulated)
Too bad I didn't bring my vibrator along—no time to pack it.

JACOB
Tina, don't worry. Where there is a will, there is a way.

TINA
Thanks.

MS. RATCHETYWRY
(re-entering the room)
Well, Jacob, some people are not doing as well as you. Today's
your big day, isn't it?

JACOB
Yes––and no. Yesterday I was only half the man I was meant to
be. Today I have a future hanging over me.
(singing, part Beatles, part Carole King, part unknown
melody)
Oh, I believe.

MS. RATCHETYWRY
Well, I'm glad you're in God spirits––I mean, *good* spirits.
Everything is in your hands now. Just see Ralph.

Jacob is seen at the desk getting his belongings from Ralph. He is holding a small plastic bag with a shirt in it.

RALPH

Here's your things.

JACOB

Ralph, I came in here with more money. I came in here with $100 that I saved from babysitting jobs.

(counting the money)

Why is this only $12.77?

RALPH

Oh come now, Jacob, God, man, or whatever you call yourself. You probably lost it in a crap game or never even had it. You're a little weird—did anyone ever tell you that? I don't think you know if you're coming or you're going. I don't even know why they're letting you out of here. Here.

(produces document)

This is your signature, see? You signed it, and it says $12.77.

JACOB

I never signed anything. Of course you forged my signature, didn't you, Ralph? I was asleep when they brought me in. I woke up... I remember now... and they shot me up with some drug. I woke up two days later. I had slept because they found me under a police station—the safest place to sleep. When I would not go with the nice men in the white jackets, when I threw them off my person, they gave me a shot in the ass of something that knocked me out'til I came here. God only knows.

RALPH

You slept like a baby. I remember. I tucked you in. I tucked you in real tight, Jacob. I don't like what you're saying. Do you want to bring this up with the hospital authorities?

JACOB
(honestly and straightforward)
No, there's no time for that. I have things to do. You needed to steal my money. Ahh, but Ralph, it is just a cry for help, isn't it? Or have you gotten yourself into some trouble? What can I do? I think it is best to give it to you without a fight. It will be very hard to help you since you are one of God's children, so deeply in a mess that only a remake would benefit you. You can have the money, and I hope you find some real peace soon, Ralph.

RALPH
(looking defensive)
You're lucky I don't report you, you psycho. But I know you're not all there.

Ralph walks away and exits.

JACOB
Well, at least I have my jacket and my change. Now I will leave enough bus fare.
(turning to his fellow patients)
Well, goodbye, my dear friends. I will always remember your love. I will always love you too.

Everyone embraces him and wishes him well.

MS. RATCHETYWRY
(embracing Jacob)
Remember, it's a cold world out there, so get a good skill and remember to stay with your friend Nero 'til you have a place of your own. Don't come back just because this is a safe place to stay. The world is waiting for you. I... I mean, there is greatness in the world, and I know you can build a life out there, Jacob.
(handing Jacob a paper bag, smiling)
This is your walking pass, Jacob.

Ms. Ratchetywry unlocks the door and lets Jacob out.

Jacob goes back to his room—a tiny space with a bed. He takes off his toga and changes into a shirt. He leaves on his earrings, looks into the mirror, and walks out the door.

CU Jacob leaving the floor and the building, showing his walking pass to a GUARD who eyes him suspiciously and then grins sarcastically. The guard is wearing a blue uniform and sits at an empty small old desk.

CUT TO:

EXT. DOWNGRADE HOSPITAL FOR THE SICK AND DEPRESSED (BROOKLYN)- DAY

As Jacob walks out of the building, there are a few bushes on each side of the exit. Jacob hears moaning of a sexual nature coming from one of the bushes. He looks down at the bushes and sees four legs: two of the legs belong to a WOMAN who is wearing high heels; the other TWO are those of a man with noticeably larger shoes. The man and woman appear to be having sexual relations in the bushes.

The guard is also watching them with much pleasure, but also looks around nervously as well. The guard remains inside the building with his nose occasionally pressing against the glass.

Only the legs of the lovers, flailing about, are visible to the camera. Their voices can be heard.

> FEMALE LOVER
> Yes, yes... that's it... no, no, we must not do it. Someone may catch us.

> MALE LOVER
> But honey lips... this has been your fantasy for years. You've been so distant, and now you're here and hot, and yes, in front of the hospital.

> FEMALE LOVER
> Well, then, *hurry*. What would my mother say if ahhh ahhh ahhh.

JACOB
(seeing the activity in the bushes)
My well, perhaps life has changed out here and now they just want to enjoy what's left.

Jacob is smiling as he moves closer to the bushes. He almost looks in and then turns away.

JACOB
(looking serious and controlled)
Well, I'll just catch that bus right over there.

EXT. BUS STOP - DAY

Jacob is at a bus stop near the hospital (or down the street a bit), waiting for the bus.

Dr. Mannose walks to the front of the building from the street. He is sucking on a beef jerky and passes by the bush where the woman is now having an orgasm. The couple in the bushes hear Dr. Mannose approach and become quiet, pulling their feet in.

Jacob is a small distance away/on the other side of the street at the bus stop, waiting for the bus under the bus stop sign.

Dr. Mannose looks at the bushes suspiciously, but then sucks on the beef snack and turns away, disinterested. He enters the building. The guard comes running out of the building, pretending to see the problem in the bushes for the first time. He is afraid Dr. Mannose saw the incident and will report him for not doing his job.

GUARD
God, what is happening here? Doctor, do you see this? Two hoodlums in the bushes. Get out of there, you perverts!

The guard runs to the bushes, looking at Dr. Mannose as often as possible.

The lovers look puffy; they're blushing. Their clothes are ripped, their hair very mussed. They are out of breath as they emerge from the bushes. The woman is wearing what is left of a short skirt and a T-shirt which reads "Shit Happens." The man is wearing a shirt that reads "Marlboro Man" (or it can be a beer ad/Budweiser shirt).

MALE LOVER

You and your fantasies—never satisfied. Well, are you satisfied now?

FEMALE LOVER

Don't blame me, you jerk! If I fell asleep doing it once with you, I fell asleep a million times. You really stink. I needed something to spice up the misery.

MALE LOVER

Women never have enough. I bought you a car... not enough. Took you to the Bahamas... not enough. Then there's kinky sex, too. Gone are the days when women were seen and not heard. Now they are heard when they're not seen. Good sex is my forte, you wild bitch! If only I left the family earlier. The crucifix on my wall was so large as a child, it kept saying "don't." What would you know of these things, having French blood on your mother's side? You're all tramps!

FEMALE LOVER

Listen, you eunuch, what would you know? Tramp is not a word for women who likes good sex. Tramp is a word for a bum like you who doesn't produce any, small stuff!

MALE LOVER

I'll give you something you can remember.

The male lover starts hitting his female lover. She strikes back; they get into a fist fight, which is more humorous than really violent.

Dr. Mannose is wearing a pin on his shirt that says "Dr. Mannose." He decides to intercede in the fight between the two lovers.

DR. MANNOSE

Stop this immediately! By coming here today, you both did a very brave thing—you exposed yourselves. All your weaknesses will be your strengths. Now go home and make a hot meal, and don't come back because this guard will have to arrest you. Okay? Now go on, and tomorrow's another day. A stitch in time saves nine, you know. Do unto others as you would have them do to you and all that.

MALE AND FEMALE LOVER

Thank you, Doctor. We didn't want to give up, anyway. We really love each other.

The lovers kiss and walk away, holding hands.

GUARD

You are a great man, Dr. Mannose. I could never handle these things as well as you. You are educated and I am not. I'm a simple man.

DR. MANNOSE

Yes, well, it's really quite simple. All men are basically without understanding of their inner potential, so you can always talk them into anything. And it took me twelve years of education to learn that, but now I know I can help people to follow the road to reason. I am retiring next year because I feel that I've done enough and I need to go on researching.

GUARD

Oh, that's wonderful.

DR. MANNOSE

Well, have a good day.

Dr. Mannose walks away, leaving the guard alone.

GUARD

(laughing to himself)

What an idiot. Oh well, it always takes time to realize that a fool with an education is more dangerous than a fool without one. He must have had some loot in his family to put him through school and pay off the teachers.

CUT TO:

INT. DOWNGRADE HOSPITAL FOR THE SICK AND DEPRESSED (BROOKLYN)

Dr. Mannose is in the hospital building, sucking on his beef jerky.

DR. MANNOSE

What a slime ball that guard is. He looks like he lives in the sewer. Those two misfits in the bushes... what slime. I only wish there was a way for me to leave this cemetery before next year. These people are beyond common—they are reptilian. Does it always have to be the same each and every day? Life with the lunatics... Buy the groceries, speak with the common angry folk. They could have been something. What a lie they are, what they could have been.

CUT TO:

EXT. BUS STOP

Jacob has grown tired of waiting for the bus; he has waited for over half an hour. He did not notice the action taking place by the hospital, and Dr. Mannose did not see him sitting on the curb waiting for the bus.

JACOB
(walking and singing)
This is ridiculous. This is not a transportation of modern man in a modern sense. A big smelly animal cracker box taking a torturous amount of time to arrive at a destination, crawling two blocks at a time. And the fare has gone up. I cannot control everything. Last time, I got locked in the bus with five boys who were swinging from the things they hold on to... um, what is it called? The thing to hold on to when the bus swings from side to side? Oh, the trains have that beat, though.
(looking saintly)
Yes, the trains have that beat. Well, it is better I walk to Nero's.
(begins singing)
What comes down must go up... for it is better to wear Oxford shoes than wide patent leathers. For he shall reign forever and

ever. Pass the latkes and the chopped liver. Natural selection has gone up the river. Pass the apple without misery. Ain't no mountain high enough to set us free.

Jacob is going to New York City by foot. He can be filmed walking over the Brooklyn Bridge (the ideal choice). If this can be done in darkness (night time), it is preferable. It is ideal to film a view of the buildings across the river, lit up and beautiful. Strong photo possibilities for this shooting. If it is not possible to do this scene in its most ideal way, then New York City is next.

EXT. THIRD STREET AND BOWERY PHONE BOOTH - NEW YORK CITY - NIGHT

It is dark and the streets are empty. Jacob is on the phone at a phone booth at the Bowery around Third Street, which it will be taking place next—with or without the bridge scene.

> JACOB
> (muttering to himself, into the phone)
These dam phones. Oh yes, operator. It's a recording. But I just put in twenty-five cents. Why wasn't I given the powers that a god should have? Okay, here's another quarter. Are you happy now, you loathsome machine?
Hello, Nero, is that you? Mrs. Trachea? Hello, how are you? Is everything okay? Should I bring anything with me? Um, um, what is that, Mrs. Trachea? I can't hear you. Well yes, you're yelling loud enough, but I can't hear you when you yell. Didn't Nero tell you that I was coming? Yes, coming tonight. No, this is not the Second Coming, Mrs. Trachea. I am not a lunatic. Yes, yes, I realize Nero is coming along now. Well, Mrs. Trachea, I had nothing to do with those fires he set in Queens. Well, I've always been a god—I mean a good influence on him. I had nothing to do with the plans he had for you and his mother last year. I encouraged him to see that he was very fortunate in having both you and his mother in a live state... and

if you remember, he did not banish you from the house either, as he had before he met me.

To tell you the truth, Mrs. Trachea, I think Nero is okay—I mean, he is a normal red-blooded American boy. He just should stop eating clay, because I think it unfocuses him. Hello... Mrs. Trachea? Hello? Oh, don't hang up. Oh damn!

I can't get to first base today, can I? I'm sure Nero meant well, but he is married to a very hard woman. I know in my heart that he is good, but if he isn't, what can I do? I grew up with him, we played softball together, and went out with the same girl in high school. He is the only one who would have me, and I will not forget his kindness.

Jacob sits on a curb with his head in his hands for a while, thinking. He is under a street light or somewhere where the light casts an interesting shadow.

> JACOB (Cont'd)
> Oh well I am blessed. If not me, then who? I will find my way through this so that I can help mankind, and I will also find my way, too.

A flood of light and shadow photography for a lengthened period.

Jacob begins to form his ideas through poetry of his own.

> JACOB (Cont'd)
> Creatures of the earth. On the great horizon. Strangled children under the feet of civilization, robbed of conscience, sight, and mind, evolve. Only fit for self-survival. Alone in thought. Nothing for the miserly souls to ache for. Tears the last trace of human life. All love must end sometime. I am always alert to the order of things.

Without advance warning, three skinheads appear in a strange, shadowy light. They are almost a full block from Jacob. He looks up as he hears their loud voices and hides behind the building.

JACOB (Cont'd)
    (thinking aloud)
Since it is obvious that I am without power these days, I better hide before I am killed by those men. If I die, I want to go a better way. In my short life, I am convinced that a god does not live forever.

The skinheads—MAGGOT, BRUNO, and PAULY—are bald and wear jackets with Nazi emblems on them. They also have tattoos; one of a snake and other reptiles are visible. They are drunk but take turns looking around once in a while. One of these men is wearing a jacket that has a man on it in a violent scene.

Jacob is hiding in or around a building close to the skinheads who reach Jacob's area too quickly and must be avoided

BRUNO
You know, we should kill that thing—whatever he is... Indian thing. Hey, listen to the lyrics of my new song—a hit. "Hey thing in a white man's world, hey thing... are you man or dog?" Ya like it?
We're gonna kill him. He wouldn't have told us to leave if that fag hadn't'a been there. You know, the pretty boy we threw over the bar... Ha ha ha ha! Yeah, what a night. He won't be sucking for a long time. After that busted lip heals, he'll remember us when he goes to the store for ice. I think those fags should be exterminated. What do you think about it? Ha ha, they would squeal a lot, I bet—just like a woman. They are just like women.

All three men are walking and almost swaying, but with a balance and toughness to their walk.

MAGGOT and PAULY
Yeah, ha ha ha ha.

MAGGOT
Yeah, but he was pretty... ha ha ha. But I like my women *without* a rod. Anyway, his tits were way too small for my

tastes—how'bout you, Pauly? You ain't feeling a liking for the boy, are you?

PAULY

You always say things 'cause you know you could get away with them, don't you, Maggot?'Cause you're my brother. Someday, I'm gonna cut the ties.

MAGGOT

How about now, big brother? How about now?

PAULY

Suits me fine, asshole. Blades okay?

BRUNO

Now boys, don't fight each other. I learned that from my teacher at the meeting, you know, "White men in a dark pit." They know what is worth fighting. You're both good, strong white boys with a brain, and you've got to fight the enemy, not each other. We have to stick together. Everyone's fucking the darkies, and there ain't gonna be a white man no more. So save your blades for the right time. And what would your mother think of you two brothers killing each other? She was the best in the neighborhood—saved all our lives a thousand times.

MAGGOT AND PAULY

Yeah.

The brothers put their knives away and smile begrudgingly at each other.

PAULY

So, Bruno, I heard you broke up with that girl you went out with. You know, the girl you went out with for a few weeks? She used to see a guy named Lenny, remember? He had a good operation, but the whole thing went bust and he was shot by the dogs. Some faggot cop shot the shit out of him.

BRUNO

(struggling to remember)

Oh yeah, that bitch—Sandy, Carol, I can't remember her name. We spent so much time sucking, I don't even remember the bitch's name. She was stupid. When she used to talk to me, I used to ask her to give me a blow job instead. And while she was down there, I used to think of what to ask her to do next. Ha ha ha.

I lost the woman I loved in a bike accident. I can't change that. We were alike, and for a bitch, she was good—like me. Tried anything once. She didn't flinch when I hit her, 'cause she was strong. She knocked over that bank years ago like it was nothing. She made them lie down, and she took everything. Man, she could cook too. I loved her and she could screw like a machine, but she knew when and where to do it.

PAULY

Don't think about it. She was good, but Bruno, there are other fish in the sea.

BRUNO

(thinks about it and shrugs his shoulders)

Probably there is another one like that. But I don't know where to find her. Anyway, that was once, long ago. I don't give a shit now. Anyway, where can we get some pussy tonight? I'm hungry.

MAGGOT

I know a girl who works at *Jerky's Bar*. She leaves every night at the same time. In another fifteen minutes, she'll be finished. Why don't we surprise her? She likes to take the back streets.

BRUNO, MAGGOT, AND PAULY

(speaking simultaneously and nodding in approval)

Yeah, ha ha ha.

Their pace picks up and they disappear down the street.

Jacob remains standing in the same spot where he hid, alone and afraid. He starts moving in place anxiously and steps on one foot with the other, shaking his head forlornly.

A few feet away, a man is sitting down on the ground with a paper coffee cup. He is a panhandler who uses the cup to beg for money and to drink coffee.

Jacob does not notice the man, but the man recognizes Jacob. He does not fully recognize him immediately. The man on the street watches Jacob for a while before approaching him. He is an old friend of Jacob's. His name is BENNY, and he speaks with a slight Jewish accent. He is dirty, disheveled, and very sleepy looking. He is intelligent as well.

Before they talk and meet, Jacob is speaking aloud to himself alone as Benny watches from a small distance. Benny appears from a light that can be seen in the street. He is walking down the street first before he sits down, and he arrives after the three skinheads are out of sight.

JACOB

Oh God, they are going to rape someone. What can I do? Un... you never get a straight answer from the cops unless you're wearing a good suit or a clean outfit. If only I had a place to clean up... but she can't be there alone when... they all said they were going to the bar—*Jerky's Bar*. Oh Christ, what can I do? I am only a man. I'm only doing what I can. I'm only able to do so much. I'm a god, too, but I seem to be powerless lately.

Jacob feels a tap on his shoulder and jumps a foot in the air. In the next moment, he recognizes his friend Benny and embraces him.

BENNY

Jacob, is that you? I should know first before I come over there to hug you. Jacob, hello? What's wrong? Have you been mugged? You look terrible. You okay? Everything all right?

JACOB

Oh, Benny, you're alive! I thought you died in high school from an overdose of quaaludes. You're alive, and I'm so glad to see you. I never needed to see anyone so much!

BENNY

You look a little pale, Jacob. You're not playing God again, I hope. Want a little coffee, Jacob?

JACOB

(sickened at the sight of the dirty coffee cup)

No, Benny, no thanks. I'm not thirsty.

(defensively but convincingly)

I'm not *playing* God! Was I *playing* God when we hung out years ago?

BENNY

It was right after your mother wanted to send you to Yeshiva, I think. First you were into drugs—like all of us. But you quit. You said back then that you couldn't remember what you were reading half the time. Remember when you got into those philosophy books—Plato and all those guys?

JACOB

Yeah!

BENNY

Remember when you decided that the world was doomed to be destroyed by mankind and you were on the high school debating team?

JACOB

Yeah!

BENNY

You won and you got to stay in a regular high school. You convinced your parents that religion was for idiots.

JACOB

Yeah!

BENNY

That's when you started believing you were God.

JACOB

Yeah.

BENNY

Well, anyway, I hope that's over with. You had the whole school in an uproar when you started having followers. I'll never forget it.

JACOB

Listen, there's no time for all that now. There's a girl, and she's in great danger. There's three skinheads who are going to attack this girl at *Jerky's Bar.* Do you know where that is?

BENNY

What do you want to know for?

JACOB

Benny, Benny... please. You don't have to come with me, just tell me what street it's on.

BENNY

Three skinheads are going to attack a woman. There isn't a policeman in the city that would listen to us. Three skinheads— and you're Jewish, Jacob. With a name like Jacob, anyone can see. And don't think they won't beat it out of you. They're big on backgrounds.

JACOB

Listen, Benny, I'm not going to tackle those thugs. I'm going to warn the lady and leave. Okay, now.. where is this place? Quickly... before she gets hurt.

BENNY

Follow me.

CU Benny and Jacob running past a street light.

FADE OUT.

FADE IN.

INT. ALL-NIGHT GROCERY STORE - LATE NIGHT

Benny and Jacob are buying food with Jacob's money. He has $12.27 left after the phone calls he made earlier. He is searching for six dollars of his money but can't find out until he remembers to look in his shoe.

> JACOB
> (looking in his shoe)
> Here, I found it. Now here's all the money we need for dinner.

> BENNY
> Let's go in here. I like their spiced ham.

> JACOB
> Okay. Do they have Hawaiian Punch?

> BENNY
> Yeah, I think so.

Ralph, the owner of the grocery store, is a kind and helpful man but is not very swift.

> RALPH
> (stupid but friendly)
> Hello, my friend. How are you, Benny? Any good numbers lately? My friend Angelo won big last week. I think maybe he won $200.

> JACOB
> (turning to Benny)
> You play the numbers?

Jacob studies Benny as if to imply that he is not in a financial situation to do so.

> BENNY
> Just a little. You gotta be in it to win it, right, Ralph?

> RALPH
> (shrugs with certainty)
> Yeah, sure.

JACOB
Ralph, your name is Ralph? I know of a Ralph. He's always betting on the numbers, but winning never does much for his moods.

RALPH
Well, boys, what will it be? I'll tell you what... tonight, I have a special on spiced ham, and I'll sell it to you for—

Jacob does not hear Ralph speak; instead, he hears music—violins or some type of classical soft music. He is mesmerized by this and does not respond until Benny taps him firmly on the shoulder.

BENNY
What's wrong, Jacob? Before you start thinking again, tell Ralph what you want. He has a special on spiced ham.

The music stops.

JACOB
Uh-oh. Yeah, that's fine... spiced ham.

BENNY
On what? Tell Ralph what you want it on.

JACOB
White bread, um…
        (rubbing his eyes)
plenty of mayo, please.

RALPH
Sure thing, buddy. You better get some sleep. You look like you could use some rest. You have a place to stay tonight, don't you?

BENNY
Oh yeah, sure we do. I have my own place. It's not a palace, but it's a house without a landlord.

CUT TO:

EXT. STREET OUTSIDE GROCERY STORE 7- NIGHT

Jacob and Benny walking together, eating and drinking.

CUT TO:

EXT. ABANDONED APARTMENT BUILDING - NIGHT

Jacob and Benny enter the abandoned building where Benny lives.

CUT TO:

INT. ABANDONED APARTMENT BUILDING- NIGHT

CU Jacob and Benny sitting inside an abandoned apartment building in candlelight. They take out plastic garbage bags to sleep on for warmth. It is completely dark except for the light from the candle.

BENNY

Well, I'm glad you talked me into that. After all, you don't save a life every day. After that lady hit us and told us to buzz off, she really came around. Imagine, giving us a hug and running off, saying that we saved her life and she'll never forget us. I always wondered why nice women like that go near those places. Well, you can't change the world, can you, Jacob?

JACOB

Yes, you can, Benny. You can—or you can die from submission. I know, Benny, that if we are only fit for self-survival, all love must end sometime.

BENNY

You know, Jacob, I got pretty tired of all the bullshit too, that's why I'm out here. But I don't get treated right, and I know if I fight back, it gets worse. But that don't worry me much because I know something that they don't know—I'm better than them more... human.

JACOB

Yeah, more human. And look at what it took to teach us. Years of living and watching loyalty run like the wind. To be mortal is to die alone. Remember the time we both ate a pound of M&M's?

BENNY

Yeah. That was after we smoked three bowls of the good stuff—
whatever that was. Ha ha, you swore off pot that day. You
thought you could fly, and then when you tested it off your
bunk bed, you fell on your back. Ha ha, and your mother took
you to the doctor and he said you were okay, so she punished
you and made you stay home. You were so miserable. You said
your old man was boring you with war stories, and your mother
was making chicken every day, and it smelled like smelly cheese.
She came home from work and you couldn't get up and she
found you, ha ha.

JACOB

She found everything—the pot and the downers.

(clears his voice in an important-sounding way)

I'm over that now. That was my earlier journey. I guess I had
to know everything that man was poisoning himself with to be
successful in my mission.

BENNY

(looking sadly at Jacob)

Oh, I see, Jacob. Well, I'm tired. Perhaps we can talk more
tomorrow. Whatever you're into, Jacob, I support you—no
matter what mishegas it is. What is truly important is that we
will always be buddies. Tomorrow we have to beg—beg for
money. Begging is my career. And it beats my old job at the
stock brokerage firm. Selling stocks was so pointless since I had
no time to enjoy the money anyway. I kept saying to myself,
"Money saved is money earned." It never meant anything to
me, facing those idiots every day, backstabbing to make a buck.
Well, hmm, goodnight, Jacob.

JACOB

Goodnight, Benny.

They both snuggle into the garbage bags as blankets. Benny falls asleep
first. Benny snores lightly and sleeps restlessly while Jacob stares at the

half-destroyed ceiling with stuffed garbage bags in the holes. Jacob falls into a deep sleep.

JACOB
(snoring lightly, talking in his sleep)
I would I would not... *zzzzzz* I All love is *zzzzz*...
(yelling)
Would you stop piling up my ass like a hemorrhoid?

BENNY
(waking up with a start)
Jacob, is someone here?

JACOB
No. It was just a dream.

BENNY
Oh, well, don't yell. You'll wake the neighbors, and I don't want any trouble from the people who live next door.

JACOB
Okay.

They both fall back asleep.

INT. ABANDONED BUILDING APARTMENT
– EARLY MORNING

Light pours in through the cracks in the ceiling. Benny is sleeping, and Jacob is awake and dusting himself off. Jacob speaks softly to himself, deep in thought.

JACOB
(to himself)
I think I'll surprise Benny and get some food without him. I could beg if I have to. Well, maybe I should go to a store and beg them. That would cut corners a little bit.

Jacob pulls out a pen and his walking pass from the hospital and writes a note to Benny on it.

CUT TO:

INT. CHICKEN RIGHT RESTAURANT - DAY

It is opening time. ARNIE BENEDICT is manager of this restaurant; he is wearing a pin which bears his name. He is alone behind the counter. He is no more than nineteen years old, has greasy curly black hair, and a very odd face; he looks like a gangster from the 1930s and looks like he is from a mobster movie. He eyes Jacob suspiciously. Jacob has gotten dirtier since the last scene and his eyes are somewhat unfocused.

                    JACOB
Hi there, Mr. Benedict. I am sure you've been asked this before, but I am very hungry, and I slept in an abandoned building last night with my friend Benny.

                    ARNIE
Oh yeah? How was he—any good?

                    JACOB
I didn't have much food last night, just a spiced ham sandwich and a Hawaiian Punch.

                    ARNIE
A spiced ham sandwich and a Hawaiian Punch? Well, you're living better than me. All I eat is this crappy chicken every day. Now, what can I do for you?

                    JACOB
     (muttering to himself)
You are not a creation I can be proud of.

                    ARNIE
What did you say, meat loaf brain?

                    JACOB
I said this restaurant is a creation to be proud of.

                    ARNIE
Don't kiss my ass, buffalo breath. I'll give you a piece of chicken, anyway. I was just gonna throw this out. It was left on a table

for two days. No one saw it. Want it? It's probably still good. I would take it if I had nothing.

JACOB

I have a friend. Could I just get two pieces?

ARNIE

I don't like greedy homeless people. I offer you one, you want two. Okay, here's two. Now, beat it, and don't come back. Remember, I don't like the spongers near my store.

JACOB
(talking to himself as he exits the store)

Obviously another mistake—faulty wiring. Almost evolved, but yet still stuck in that developmental stage of half *Homo sapiens* and half **C** ro-Magnon. I wonder what the missing link is like. I don't think Benny will mind if I eat my piece without him.

CUT TO:

EXT. STREET OUTSIDE CHICKEN RIGHT - DAY

Jacob eats and is seen making faces of disgust, but he eats quickly, somehow believing that it will fill him up and make the experience pass quickly. He's still talking to himself.

JACOB (Cont'd)

Ugh, tastes just like my mother's chicken used to—real disgusting with that lingering cheese taste. Smelly cheese. It just might be that my mother passed away from her own cooking. I should have dragged her out of the kitchen, even though she insisted on doing all the cooking. I should have bodily thrown her out.

Ugh, this is disgusting! My father made eggs, and he was proud of how perfect they were. What a pair. Well, I came out of it. I need some water.

As Jacob walks, he appears to be getting sick. He sits down and holds his head.

JACOB (Cont'd)
That chicken—why did I eat it?

People pass Jacob and look at him for a second and quickly turn away, disinterested. One woman looks at Jacob with sympathy then continues to walk away.

JACOB (Cont'd)
(talking to himself)
Oh, I have a headache. Now I've done it.

He looks at a drugstore and walks over to it.

CUT TO:

EXT. DRUG STORE WINDOW - DAY

There is a bottle of aspirins in the window. Jacob begins to smile; he imagines the tablets are coming out of the aspirin bottle.

He speaks to himself slowly. With excitement, he imagines the aspirin tablets flying slowly out of the bottle in the window and growing large. Suddenly, he looks Christlike.

JACOB
Ahh, the tablets are coming out. The tablets are getting bigger, out, out, out of the aspirin bottle. Great big tablets. I see it. At last I see it. The truth is written on the tablets. Commandment 1 says: man, woman, dogs, cats, bugs were created with a brain and a heart. Everybody has feelings. Man sometimes has feelings too. If your heart hurts, cushion yourself with your arm. If your arm aches, seek refuge in the fly overhead. If the fly does not bring comfort...
(sighing)
lie down and dream. Yes, if your dream is to build a hill, build it as high as your strength allows. Aspirins, mmmm, if there is love in your life, build a mountain effortlessly.

A crowd has gathered, but they are unsure of whether to listen or walk away.

JACOB (Cont'd)
Ahh, now Commandment 1 $\frac{1}{2}$ and 2 $\frac{1}{2}$—

The crowd laughs uneasily.

JACOB (Cont'd)
The tablet says do not steal from the poor to give to yourself. Do not sell your mother-in-law into slavery—even if they promise to let her outlive her usefulness.

The small crowd nods in approval, and the laughter is no longer heard, except for one young girl. Jacob holds his head, thinking.

JACOB (Cont'd)
Above all, don't become a Republican. It is harder for a Republican to see the light of a sunny day than it is for a snake to say "Good morning, how would you like your toast?" Give the odd guy a chance, slim.

Two men who were listening start walking away in thought.

JACOB (Cont'd)
You cannot understand. That tablet isn't so clear. Oh yeah, you cannot understand the poor, the sick, and the aged, and not the different man. Or the... the same man, when he is different.
(he looks back at Chicken Right)
Oh, it's good. They won't let me... back. No living gods allowed. Now, what was I saying?

A YOUNG WOMAN, about sixteen years old, has been listening to Jacob. She responds.

YOUNG WOMAN
The same man when he is different.

JACOB
Oh yes. The original chicken and the crispy chicken. Oh, let us say on a day when only hot wings are served by a tired and angry

chicken clerk, we must understand he does not like loonies in his store. Um, understand your fellow man. What is evident...
(sitting down and looking up to the sky)
is only part of the struggle.

An OLDER WOMAN who has been listening joins in.

OLDER WOMAN
Amen.

JACOB
What is evident is only part of the struggle in a human predator evolving to his natural end—or to a new beginning, if we know which way is up. Our morality is our mortality, the alarm clock. Time is so scarce.

OLDER WOMAN AND YOUNGER WOMAN
(simultaneously)
Yes.

The two women look at each other and slowly walk away.

JACOB
You must see what is valuable in our short life, and... and what are just bridge tolls to get to the other side of the you that is moral and can reason. Without um...
(he looks at his feet)
both reasoning and morality, you might risk your life to save a soda can being hurled in the air toward the sea.
(massaging his foot as he speaks)
It is too bad the dog has more sense and personality. He always knows where to pee and... when to run in the snow.
(looks at his feet and then to the sky)
Commandment no. 3—never say no to an idea that has merit.

He lies down in a fetal position in front of the closed store where he has been giving this sermon.

JACOB (Cont'd)

Commandment no. 4—in loving those who have less, you are beautiful to behold. Life is short, live it to the fullest.

He closes his eyes and lies there quietly. No one is listening; feet can be seen passing him.

A MAN and WOMAN, arm in arm, walk close to Jacob; they make no attempt to help him even though the woman wants to.

MAN

Watch out, honey. Those people urinate everywhere.

WOMAN

Oh, John, you can really upset me sometimes. What if he's dead? Should we call someone?

MAN

They'll find him.

WOMAN

Should I leave a dollar by him? Maybe he just passed out.

MAN

No, he might be dangerous. Never give those people money unless their cup is out.

They walk away.

MONTAGE

Photography captures curious stares for some minutes and the city life and buildings. CU on Jacob as he rises very slowly. He stretches, as if awakening from a deep sleep. He looks as though everything is quite normal; he cracks (or tries to crack) his knuckles.

JACOB

Well, Jacob Paul Buddaman, this certainly has been some day. I feel better already. Benny must be worried about me. I better get back, and with nothing for him to eat.

Jacob shakes his head sadly and walks away. Light or sunlight is upon him. He is shot in an angle that adds height to him and adds magnificence to his presence as he walks down the street.

BLACK OUT.

The numbers "2093" appear in large illuminated white type on the screen. The scene opens in the year 2093.

FADE OUT.

FADE IN.

EXT. CHICKEN RIGHT RESTAURANT

Very slow and carefully pan on the building, giving the viewer a slow study. The entrance is the same in appearance as it was in 1993.

Above the entrance is a gold plaque reading Chicken Right 1993–2093: A Century of Good Living.

Four men construction workers are working in front of the restaurant. Two of the men are drilling the sidewalk with a light-looking instrument that resembles the drill. This tool makes no sound and does not weigh enough to make a sound when dropped. The two men drilling are named PEDRO and JUNIOR. Pedro is Hispanic and Junior is very fair skinned. They are both very attractive. Junior occasionally reminds one of Laurel of the Laurel and Hardy comedy team of the 1930s; he often moves and expresses himself like Laurel, although he has, at the same time, a sexy quality about him.

The two construction workers sitting down are named RICHARD and KEVIN; they are eating lunch from lunch boxes that are of a metal appearance and look exactly like the lunch pails men used for outside work in the 1950s. Richard and Kevin are attractive as well.

They all wear bandannas to hold their hair back. The bandannas are blue and white, the same as we see people wearing today.

Pedro leans on the drill with his arm and wipes sweat from his brow with a handkerchief.

An ATTRACTIVE FEMALE walks by and pinches Pedro on the backside.

ATTRACTIVE FEMALE

How about a little something for your mamma?

She laughs heartily and walks in a lively step down the street.

Pedro holds the drill insecurely with one hand, and the handkerchief is rolled into a ball in his other hand. He speaks defensively to the attractive female as she walks away.

PEDRO

Leave me alone!
(to the men)
When are they going to stop doing that? I work all day in the hot sun, only to be a toy to some idiot woman—some woman that looks at me like I'm a piece of meat. When are they going to learn that I'm a man? I'm more than an object they can manipulate and use. I'm quitting today.
(throws down drill, which makes no sound)
Shit, I've had enough.

Junior falls in and out of Laurel schtick. He's sexy one moment, then smiles stupidly and scratches his head like Laurel. Suddenly, he seems to be thoughtful and concerned.

JUNIOR

Don't let them get to you like that. Act tough and removed like you know you are, buddy.
(acts intelligent and sexy for a moment only)
The minute you say something to them, it turns them on. Like don't say "leave me alone."

(scratches head)

That only makes them bother you more. Maybe even bring back friends...

(grins with assurance)

or tell some other women where you are, and you're going to be here for a while.

(leans forward, looking like
Laurel in a moment of passion)

Don't walk out.. fight this.

KEVIN AND RICHARD

(rising, patting Pedro on the back to comfort him)

Yeah!

KEVIN

When it happens to me, I just take them on. I say, "Listen, sister," and "I'll tell you something that will make your head spin." I tell them I'm not interested.

RICHARD, PEDRO, JUNIOR

(listening closely, sing-song simultaneously)

Does it work?

KEVIN

(thoughtful and sad)

Well... well you know, with the war on and all, so many of our good women have been drafted... I get lonely. I served my time.

(sadly)

Lord only knows, I'm past the age to go in again. But sometimes... I wish I could join up so I could meet some decent women with family values.

PEDRO

Yeah, you're right. Life goes on. I'll fight it out. After all, I got to keep up with my ex-wife. She's always buying the kids better things.

(whining just a little)

She got that job, and now life's crazy. Well, I hope at least they relocate her to Florida like they were promising.

JUNIOR
Well, guys, let's finish up so we could get out of here.

They all begin drilling the sidewalks with the drills that make no sound and have strange lights blinking.

CUT TO:

EXT. STREET - DAY

CU TWO CHILDREN running with toy guns. The toy guns are very futuristic. One child, the brother, is seven; the sister is about nine years old.

Angle on their MOTHER chasing children down the street. She is dressed in a halter top and is wearing sunglasses that are very dark. She is out of breath and spits on the sidewalk.

BOY
It's not over 'til the last man is dead. I will terminate you. I will kill kill kill.

The boy holds the gun in the air and lets out a yell. He then points it at his sister, who is farther up the block.

BOY (Cont'd)
Have you ever died this way?

He runs into the area where the construction men are working and accidentally crashes into Pedro.

Pedro, at this moment, is picking up a paper he dropped out of his shirt pocket. He bends down to pick it up and falls flat on his face in an area of wet cement when the boy runs into him.

He gets up slowly but cannot rise at first. CU Pedro's face with cement covering everything but his eyes. He wipes his face, his eyes bulging out of his head with fury. He is lying on the ground, still.

CUT TO:

The boy runs faster, but not with too much concern. He apologizes to Pedro and runs after his sister.

          BOY

Sorry.

The boy skips on, his mother in hot pursuit.

          MOTHER

Get back here, you two. Did you bump into that man? Idiot!

          GIRL
            (skipping, yelling to Boy)

Get a life!

She runs faster away from her brother, snickering.

          BOY

It's not over 'til the last man is dead.

The boy shoots at his sister. The girl shoots him with a toy gun and aims for his head, looking like a real hit woman. She looks proud and happy.

          GIRL
            (snickering)

Yeah, well, I'm not playing. I'm always the last man.

          BOY

The last man is dead, shithead.

The boy shoots his sister and looks satisfied.

The mother catches up to them.

          MOTHER

Stop that, both of you. Where did you ever learn to act that way? You always act like a pair of idiots. Did I raise you to talk that way in the street? Look at you—dirty already. Such slobs! Did I raise you to act like two pigs rolling in the dirt constantly?
            (spits on sidewalk)
I'm telling your father whenever he gets home. He'll take the belt out and teach you a lesson.

(seeing an ice cream parlor)
That's all I have to say for now. Let's get some ice cream and go home.

> BOY and GIRL
> (angelically)
Yes, Mamma.

FADE OUT.

FADE IN.

EXT. WASHINGTON SQUARE PARK - DAY

Two young people are walking by Washington Square Park. VINCENT is a young man, black, twenty-three years old, and reminds one of Jacob Paul Buddaman, seen earlier in this story. He is carrying books—philosophy books of great philosophers of positive thinking. He is wearing a cellophane suit and black shorts underneath that go to his knees.

DELORES is the woman with Vincent. She is dressed in cellophane as well. She is carrying books from college as well. She is also around twenty-three years old.

> VINCENT
Professor Bellvue is so right. Mankind is hanging on by a thread. I am a firm believer in the might and meaning of science. After all, it has given women the chance to unite with their husbands in the reunion chamber. Perhaps the only good thing to come out of thought replica stations these days is the human love we so desperately try to hide from one another. The hate though that the thought replica brings to the surface of the evil minded is the problem! Perhaps man was better off with his little box in the past—you know, telviser or something.

> DELORES
You don't remember what it was called? It was called television—a simple way to entertain the people that lived back then. It at

least kept the crime rate down to a murder every few minutes because people could watch violent acts in their homes instead of the portable headset that the thought replica has. Now people get so turned on to murder, and they fantasize as they go. That's what I've heard, at least.

VINCENT

Really? That's terrible. What is the world coming to? Well, I have found my real peace with the Amen Mena Pause religion, a religion totally accepting of science. It actually is not based on biblical creation, and the belief is not that man is separate from the animals in his development. It simply has four commandments, and the commandments are so wonderful, so much what man has been waiting for. They were all found on tablets one hundred years ago by our Lord, Jacob Paul Buddaman.

DELORES

What kind of tablets?

VINCENT

Actually, I have heard his vision came to him by a drugstore. Um, actually, they were giant aspirin tablets.

DELORES

Do they want any money?

VINCENT

No.

DELORES

Do they want you to join a cult, you know, shave your head or something?

VINCENT

No.

DELORES

Well, be careful.
    (affectionately)
You know what I mean.

She hugs him lightly.

VINCENT

Don't worry, this is the real thing—no fraud. They ask nothing of me but to be moral. That's easy enough. No other rules. And you know what's wonderful? We meet in the park, Washington Square Park, once a week on Wednesday, and we all sit in a big circle and discuss how we're going to change the world for the better. There are only about one hundred of us now, but we're growing. Three girls from parochial school just joined us. Would you like to come on Wednesday?

DELORES

I'll think about it. I don't think so. I've been a Buddhist for years. Well, I have to run. I have to meet my mom at the airport. She's coming in from Long Island. See ya.

VINCENT

Bye, take care.

CUT TO:

INT. CHICKEN RIGHT RESTAURANT- EARLY EVENING- SAME DAY

The manager at the counter is nineteen years or so. He is wearing a pin that says "Manager, Arnie Barnacle." He is the same Arnie as in 1993 and he wears the same uniform, except he has gray hair. Grease is on the tables and counter. There is a sign to form a line at the counter.

RUTH SHLEPER enters. She is attractive, in her thirties, and somewhat nervous. She is grabbing a bite at Chicken Right before working at the Squarebud Theatre, where she is a telemarketer. She is a single woman and frustrated with the single life. Although her troubles are clear, her delivery is somewhat on the comical side.

Ruth has just finished an acting class and is sharing her experience with Vincent, the student who is a member of the Amen Mena Pause religion. It is Wednesday, the meeting night for Amen Mena Pause. He is grabbing a bite with Ruth before the services in the park start.

RUTH
(entering restaurant with Vincent)
What bullshit! That instructor doesn't know the first thing about acting. Did you hear him read his lines?

VINCENT
Yes. Well, he did a very good "official in the White House treaty-signing" scene. He looked very serious and seemed focused on the moment when he said, "Sign at the dotted line, and don't read the print again. We'll miss the flag ceremony at Quayle's house. The barbecued chicken there is always so good."

RUTH
Well, he forgot these lines too, remember?

VINCENT
That is because it was close to the end of class. You know he has to remind us to stop at the receptionist's desk every week to pay. We need our receipts to enter class each week. Some people have been leaving without paying. Jack said it was his way of seeing when he would really want to pay. If he leaves three times without paying, he's not coming back.

RUTH
Well, at least they got their money's worth.

She leans on the counter, thinking.

ARNIE
May I help you folks? Is my clock wrong, or have you been standing here
(slaps his hand on counter and hits soda spill)
… in this same spot on my serving line for at least ten minutes?

He wipes hands his a little like Hardy would, although not kind in any way.

RUTH
(said cautiously)
Well, there is no one here on this line but us.

Vincent nods his head in agreement.

ARNIE
(throwing a rag on counter)
It is a fact that you and you alone are on this line. But would you do this in another restaurant—perhaps one more suitable to the sensitive pallet? Do not fear.

A dog barks OC (and cannot be seen).

ARNIE (Cont'd)
We are quite prepared for your arrival. Fe Fe will show you to a lovely table in the rear, where you will be presented with the finest in hamburger cooking. We are noted for our chili burgers. Fe Fe is, of course, a dog, I must admit, but a good one. She understands the burger better than you or I. Now what can I do for you? We have no chicken today.

VINCENT
Well, I don't know. I really was in the mood for chicken. I mean, I saw the sign *Chicken Right*, um, on the store.

Vincent moves a short step back instinctively and looks very aware of what will happen by eye contact with Arnie.

Arnie leans forward very close and comically, like Moe of the Three Stooges would to Curly or Larry. He leans forward to Vincent and meets his eyes.

ARNIE
I suppose you'd like me to go and shoot a chicken for you. Bam! Out of the sky—one satisfied customer! Well, I'm out of chicken, and that is that. The precinct came here last night, the worst night of my life. They ate 693 chickens—mainly wings. They were chasing some gang—homicidal maniacs, you know,

the elementary school blade boys. Six schools at war for their territory. The old story. Everybody wants the part of the school yard with the bases and away from the street. You know, they're tired of losing the ball and running out for it. The things that didn't bother us when we were kids! So they decided to go to war. I think there was a kindergarten class handing out cookies. I heard all this'cause after the cops left, the gangs came in.

(getting angry again)

And you want chicken.

VINCENT

No, no. I don't want chicken.

RUTH

We'll just take a, um, a delicious burger and a caffeine hit.

VINCENT

Yeah, that's right. Whatever you have... um, whatever she has, I'll have.

After passing and checking out three dirty tables, they both sit at a table and begin eating and talking.

RUTH

So how have you been, Vincent? I mean, how's your love life? Any luck with Delores?

VINCENT

Well, I'm confused. She seems to care about me, but she never acts interested in me—at least, I don't see an interest in me the way I have for her. I'm not going to bring it up yet. I want to give it time. How's your love life? Any better?

RUTH

My life is a nightmare. I can't meet a guy. They're all into weird tripys. I don't feel comfortable anywhere. And the more nervous I get about how to act with guys—guys I don't even like but feel I need to give a chance to, oh because... you know, frankly, Vincent, I am getting um, desperate... I mean, I'm thirty-five years old and I don't even have a love life. I haven't dated more than three guys in two years. One of them had a shirt on that said "No one home" and didn't talk all night. One dated me because I'm Jewish, and he wanted to please his mother. I know his mother. And one doesn't speak any English and kept saying, "Wanna make out? Wanna make out?" I really didn't like him, but I almost went home with him. Mood cushions and thought replicas do no good anymore. What is going on?

Ruth looks outside the window and sees a man passing. She becomes aroused but continues the conversation with Vincent.

VINCENT
I think the problem is that we all have a history of abusing each other. Don't you think?

RUTH
Yes, I think we do. But I hate to pay for all the abuse I didn't commit and then know that the guilty parties had so much more fun than I did.

VINCENT
Women and men are not honest with each other today. I'm reading this book—well, actually, a few books—for my history class. And in some ways, things haven't changed. My focus for the next paper is on the relations of men and women in the twentieth century. It's like the old story my grandfather told. He said when he was a boy, his father used to get attention from people passing on the street by yelling a word at them. But it never quite worked.

RUTH
What was that word?

VINCENT
Honky.

RUTH
What does it mean?

VINCENT

It means "silly white person," I think. I don't know exactly. My father always laughs when he tells that story. His father and his father before him lived in a time when poor people were even less respected than they are today. Poor black people were respected less than that. The world of the poor was the haven of the rich since drug dealers fed off the remains of hope swallowed up.

In the twentieth century, lots of people felt that lack of education was the true test of intelligence. They didn't put much stock in change, and confidence was also swallowed up in the demands of a recession. Jobs were scarce, and the lucky few held on to them tightly. Training workers ended about that time, since it wasn't necessary with thousands of people coming to job interviews. Day care did not work with the schedules my family needed.

My grandfather was a great comedian, but the big break was too far away. He needed quick answers first. It seems, from what I've read, that women suffered in the twentieth century as much as they had before the twentieth century, but in very different ways. In that day and age, people were beginning to feel like a man in the street without a prayer.

I read that for millions of years—not hundreds but millions—women were giving credit for things they thought of themselves to men in exchange for love. Men of the past would not love the women most of the time without credit for everything that was achieved. The way to ensure that dinner conversation led to the man's advancement, for example, was to use their wives' ideas and take all the credit always.

This was easy enough to do. Women had no education, no human rights, and no opportunity to say the last word. They were told that by living this way, they were the model woman. Also, if they were not virgins, they could kiss this love good-bye. Amazing, isn't it?

RUTH

Amazing.

VINCENT

In the 1960s, men and women saw a light to freedom. In the 1960s, that was chapter three, I believe. Everyone who was so repressed and knew it protested. Still, there were confusing things going on. I read that self-help books were very popular then. Psychologists and other thinkers of the period wrote these self-help books to help women. But I looked in the library, and they are very confusing. I mean the two I looked at. They seem to be written to help women say what they are feeling without really saying it.

RUTH

Hmm, that's interesting. What did they do, write them a letter?

VINCENT

No. They lied to them and continued to give them the credit. So men were trying at that time to understand what the women were feeling, but they couldn't. They themselves had been victims of a brainwashing that left them with less analytical powers than modern man can afford to have. They had been playing center field for so long, they didn't know how to play the outfield. Women were also reading too many self-help books, and they were confusing them, I imagine.

CUT TO:

CU Arnie as he sprays bug spray in the food area behind his counter and goes unnoticed by Ruth and Vincent. Arnie is also slapping bugs with a fly swatter.

CUT TO:

Vincent and Ruth are still discussing the twentieth-century woman.

RUTH

Who told you this?

VINCENT

My great-grandfather. He told me when I was a little boy, after Great-Grandma died.

RUTH

Oh.

VINCENT

Nature played a nasty trick on all of us—hormonally, that is. In *Enslavement of the Twentieth Century*, I read people were so affected by their moods that they suffered terribly. No mood cushions then. Men would kill deer...

(shakes his head)

and hang them up on the wall—the head only—along with other creatures they had killed.

Loud police car sirens echo obtrusively. Vincent waits until the sound trails off.

VINCENT (Cont'd)

No hormonal retrievers then. Women were at the mercy of their bodies as well. Throughout the twentieth century, some women had severe premenstrual syndromes. During this time, it is said that women always said what they felt and men always listened. My family has laughed about what Great-Grandma did to Great-Grandpa for so many years.

RUTH

What did she do?

Arnie is content after killing some flies and begins to nod off to sleep. He is asleep at the counter during the conversation between Vincent and Ruth.

VINCENT

Well, she asked him a question while he was watching that televisor... um, television. He didn't answer, so she put his dinner in the garbage and went to bed. When he went to bed and fell asleep hours later—he was supposed to be a very heavy sleeper—she tied his leg to the bedpost with a sheet, rolled the bed over to the window, and shifted him out.

RUTH

Oh my god, were they high up?

VINCENT

Yes, but she let him right back in as soon as he answered the question. That's nothing. I heard from my family that this woman—I think it was in the 1990s—put shavings in his meatballs and used it as bread crumbs.

RUTH

Yuck, that is so disgusting! Shavings of what?

VINCENT

Her leg hairs. They used to shave their legs back then.

RUTH

How silly.

VINCENT

So you're not as unlucky as you think. You at least know who you are.

RUTH

I am a free woman on an island.

Arnie, still sleeping with his head on the counter, is snoring lightly. As Ruth says the word "island," he snorts loudly.

VINCENT

The problems that we have may be solved in time for our happiness to be more than just a passing thrill on the mood cushion. With all this change we have undergone as a civilization, you'd think that the repressed would be humans that have born-again humanity. People have not all changed for the better over the century. From what I can see, many of the people who have suffered and struggled for their rights have gone from being repressed to repressing others. Many people have not brought along their concern for suffering and have not brought more kindness and patience into the world. The men of the past are no different than many of the people of today. Most people seem to be interested in one thing—

RUTH AND VINCENT
(simultaneously)
Money!

Sirens sound again; they are both silent until the sound has dissipated.

RUTH
Well, I have had a bad life in the love arena for twenty years now. Sometimes I think that I ask too many questions, sometimes not enough. But I have nothing to lose that will... well, surprise me. At least I know I'm not alone. All my friends are going through this. Medicine and quacks are keeping me going. Anyway, don't ask me about the auditions. Tonight, I will speak my mind to the man I at least know I am attracted to and speaks to me occasionally. I will ask him everything that I've been meaning to and get it all out in the open.

VINCENT
Good idea. No need to be like the women of the past, you know, always looking for approval to say what you want to.

The woman and children with guns who were seen on the street earlier enter. The woman speaks to Arnie, who remains sleeping.

WOMAN
Hey, jerk, wake up. You got customers.

The children are sticking their fingers up each other's noses.

Ruth is unaware of their presence; she is very engrossed in her conversation with Vincent.

RUTH
Well, are you going to the Squarebud Theatre tonight to sell, sell, sell on the phone to theatergoers?

(she chuckles)

Or should I say from the deadbeats that are the theater world? That's where he is—the golden boy. Sometimes, I think I'm so attracted to him because he's so different than me. I've seen him on my thought replica for weeks now. He is in the Squarebud Theatre every night, selling. He's right next to me by the garbage can and the pole.

The woman with children continues trying to get Arnie's attention. He is waking up slowly.

WOMAN

What are you on? It's obviously not a stimulator.

VINCENT

Oh, that's him. He looks just like um... yeah, he looks like Clint Westwood, but is he interested in anything you're interested in?

Ruth does not speak; she just thinks in a very thoughtful way.

ARNIE

(to the woman)

Very funny, lady.

(sees the children and suddenly looks frightened and respectful)

Well, I'm very sorry. Worked really hard last night. What would you like? Um, um, we have no chicken. But everything for children is on special discount prices.

WOMAN

Yeah? Well, I don't see a thing on your wall for children.

Her daughter, the little girl, takes out the toy gun that up until now has been in one of her pockets; she begins massaging it while looking dangerously at Arnie.

ARNIE

(looks afraid, speaking rapidly)

Well, everything here is 50 percent off—no matter what it is. In fact, this is Family Day, and anyone with a family can get all our food for free. Just today. I forgot all about it.

MOTHER
(to children)
Order whatever you want, kids, and take plenty of napkins, too.
(the girl complies)
Good girl, honey.

Vincent and Ruth stare at the woman and children as they sit a few seats away. The family is unwrapping their food and eating.

GIRL
(to boy)
You're so stupid, you need a brain from a rabbit to make you smarter.

BOY
(to girl)
You're so stupid, a rabbit has a bigger brain than you. You have the cranial capacity of a bird.

MOTHER
Where'd you learn all that shit? Be quiet and eat before I take you home.

Ruth and Vincent turn away from the family and look at each other. Ruth speaks to Vincent.

RUTH
Well, he's an actor. Other than that, he never talks, so I don't know. But he has looked at me after asking me questions—you know, when he's selling on the phone or he forgets what plays the playhouse is showing. He asks me, I hang up with any customer I'm talking to and tell him. Sometimes, I call my customers back and apologize and tell them the phone line was faulty. He looks at me a little whenever he asks me any questions. You going to the Squarebud tonight?

VINCENT
Well, I'm not going tonight. Um, Ruth, are you sure this guy is interested in you?

RUTH

No.

VINCENT

Well, be careful. You remember what you did years ago with that psych professor.

RUTH

Yeah, but he asked me to tie him up.

CUT TO:

Arnie looks at Ruth with interest. He has heard nothing else they said about Ruth's love life.

VINCENT

I have a very important meeting at Washington Square Park. It's hump day, you know. I mean Wednesday and the Amen Mena Pause Society meets again for its discussion on birth control. We meet every Wednesday... and discuss the ideas of our great savior, Jacob Paul Buddaman. Tonight we will discuss the child in a repressive home environment.

CUT TO:

Vincent and Ruth both look silently over at the table where the mother and children sit. (They look for a moment only.)

VINCENT (Cont'd)

Some of our greatest thinkers have never reached the heights they were meant to reach. It is not finances that holds the family back from living the fullest life, in fact, finances are rarely the problem. Direction is. It is an old story that a child molested will be more likely to molest. There are plenty of people without money who have everything. Some people, perhaps like myself, think money is actually destructive to that wisdom. It is not a right to raise a child if you need to learn what life is really about, or let us say you don't want a child.

CUT TO:

Arnie is at the counter, looking at the front door. A HOMELESS MAN lingers and then enters.

ARNIE

Oh no, another loser. Why were those people born? They're such a waste.

HOMELESS MAN

(to Arnie)

Hi there. I'm sure you've been asked this before, but I'm very hungry, and I slept in an abandoned building with my friend.

ARNIE

Oh yeah? How was he—any good?

HOMELESS MAN

I didn't have much food last night, just uh, uh... a spiced ham. What made me say that?

ARNIE

A spiced ham sandwich, I suppose?

HOMELESS MAN

Yeah?

ARNIE

Well, you're living better than me.

Vincent, hearing this conversation, rises quickly from his seat and goes up to the homeless man and hands him his burger. He speaks to Arnie while also muttering to himself.

VINCENT

Oh, stop the music... this has probably been happening for millions of years. A guy has no money, so he starves to death, justified by people who think the person without clothes or a home should go out and just get a good job.

Vincent looks angrily at Arnie.

HOMELESS MAN

Thank you for your kindness. Worse than the hunger is the loneliness.

VINCENT

Here is a card with some better options, some better places you can stay.

HOMELESS MAN

Thanks, you're an angel. I'll never forget your kindness.

VINCENT
    (suddenly looks saintly)

It is my pleasure.

HOMELESS MAN

Yes, your pleasure to understand the different man. Good-bye.

The homeless man exits the restaurant.

Arnie suddenly looks very much like Oliver Hardy.

ARNIE

I'm not running a charity restaurant here. What are you people— yappies or something? I don't like trouble in my restaurant. I'll thank you to take your business elsewhere.

RUTH AND VINCENT
    (simultaneously)

Well, that will be fine.

They leave, shaking their heads and laughing. On their way out the door, they both belch loudly.

CUT TO:

EXT. STREET OUTSIDE CHICKEN RIGHT

Ruth accidentally steps on Pedro's foot as he drills outside the restaurant.

RUTH

Oh, I'm sorry.

PEDRO

It's okay. I'm used to it now.

Ruth smiles politely and walks away with Vincent.

A BOY NAMED SUE is dressed in a leather jacket and has his hair slicked back; he is about thirteen years old. He enters Chicken Right, walks up to Arnie, and pulls out a real gun. He puts the gun and his face close to Arnie.

> BOY NAMED SUE
>
> For Christ's sakes, Barnacle, give me all your loot—all of it.

> ARNIE
>
> (very scared)
>
> Of course. Here it is, every penny

Arnie loads money from cash register into the paper bag

> BOY NAMED SUE
>
> Just remember... when those cops start asking questions, tell'em a boy named Sue did it. Get that? Sue is my name.

Boy Named Sue leaves.

Arnie wipes sweat from his brow, breathes in and out, and regains his composure.

> ARNIE
>
> Well, another robbery. Good thing I bought the shield. My body is protected, except for my head. I always worry about that. Little bastards. Hmmm, a boy named Sue. Must be one of those swishers. Well, he'll have his way once he's in the big house. Ha ha ha.

A large metal pot hits Arnie on the head. It falls from a rack overhead. A large bang can be heard. Arnie falls fast behind the counter and is knocked unconscious.

CUT TO:

INT. SQUAREBUD THEATRE TELEMARKETING OFFICE

Angle on Ruth, PETER, and JIM, telemarketers sitting at a long, narrow table with telephones and literature in front of them. They phone theatergoers to see if they can sell tickets and subscriptions. The manager, RHONDA INKWELL, is watching at a small distance to see what the telemarketers are doing.

Rhonda is in her thirties; she is self-motivated with next to no feeling for her employees. She is conservative in dress.

HAROLD HARVEED III, the financial director, is carrying on other business. He is walking from room to room with a financial balance sheet in his hands. The sheet has many numbers on it. He is in his forties, also self-absorbed, and he wears a fitted black garbage bag for a shirt and long white pants. He is always followed by his two male assistants—THEODORE WINCE and ROGER WRIGHT. They wear blue garbage bag tops and gray pants. They walk in a line behind him as he leaves and enters each room, opening the doors he bangs shut behind him.

Harold shuts the doors with a loud, but not piercing bang each time he leaves a room. three young women—MARJORIE LONG, MARCIA HARBOR, and MARY SCOTT II also assist the him. They seem to be walking in the opposite direction of Harold, Theodore, and Roger. They all walk with purpose yet are without concern for others.

They are all without the slightest feeling for the true meaning of theater. They are snobs who have the best education money can buy. Although one would think that they are better suited for business in other areas, they are somehow attracted to the theater world.

    JIM

Ruth, I was looking over these objections. You know the customer is never going to believe that we have the best offer in town. I mean I myself fall asleep every time they show a comedy.

    RUTH

    (staring at Jim with attraction)

Yes, yes I know. But some people like the shows. They do keep coming back and letting themselves in for more.

RHONDA
(in passing, speaking without feeling)
Jim, Ruth, please let us get some subscriptions before we talk.

PETER
What does this say, Jim? You see, here... where it says that the first three plays will be cancelled, does it have the replacements available?

JIM
(suddenly very spacey in thought)
I don't know. I'm new here... you better ask Ruth.

RHONDA
(speaking to Harold in the reception area)
Well, I'm having a rough day.
(looks at nails to see if they're shaped)
These telemarketers are all the same—struggling actors who won't produce enough to keep them alive for their next show. I need some people that could sell. Last year, our ad read clearly enough. "Salesperson who can knock the socks off theatergoers." Then you know, salary and incentives.

Harold and Rhonda stare at the telemarketers with superiority.

HAROLD
Well, I should think that would help.

RHONDA
Well, of course it was just a lot of work. Four thousand applicants and imagine this: only four of them would work for twenty dollars an hour. So if that's under minimum wage, they could always earn something on the 1 percent commission. They sell five subscriptions and get 1 percent commission. I think that's fair.

HAROLD
Where could they do better?

Rhonda and Harold shake their heads silently in agreement.

Harold looks at the note and calls his staff; they're only three feet away.

HAROLD
Theodore Wince, Roger Wright, Marjorie Long, and Marsha Harbor, and of course, Mary Scott, I'm calling a meeting.

All five assistants—Theodore, Roger, Marjorie, Marsha, and Mary come to him quickly, notebooks in hand, looking to him as though he was a god.

Harold smiles at them as though they were his children but adults at the same time.

HAROLD
Very good.

The assistants walk to a room behind Harold until they reach the room and close the door behind them.

Back at the telemarketing table, everyone is busy on the phone.

RUTH
If I get one more answering machine, I'll scream. It's like this every year this time. They all go away to someplace with no theaters probably.

JIM
(staring aimlessly, his eyes drawn to the phone dial)
Yes, well perhaps they have their own little tragedies and comedies to perform—I know I do. Life is never dull when you're without your wings.

RUTH
(looks at him dreamily)
Jim, I didn't know you were so gifted in the world of poetry. In the world of thought, perhaps there is no one quite like you.

Ruth looks dreamily at Jim with her hand under her chin.

Jim begins making up poetic sentences to Ruth.

JIM

I live in a body I cannot call my own. In a world of confusion without a chicken bond... I mean bone. Yet all the things I've yet to see are waiting on that side. In a pond of like fish or a river with a beaver dam.

RUTH
(confused but still somewhat attracted)
Jim, let's talk about something else... something that's been on my mind.

Rhonda approaches the table, hands on hips.

Peter has been studying lines from a scene book. He is an actor; he recites a line he has tried to memorize then drops the book by his feet when he sees Rhonda approach the table.

PETER
I cannot tell a lie to you. I cannot lie to you.

He drops the book.

RHONDA
Need I remind you that this is a theater, not a social club? We need forty-five sales from you each evening to justify your existence. There are plenty of people waiting for your job out there.

Rhonda points to the door as Jim, Ruth, and Peter nod their heads in unison.

JIM, RUTH, PETER
(simultaneously)
Yes, Ms. Inkwell.

RHONDA
Now I understand this is hard work, that's why you have been chosen out of four thousand applicants. Prove that you are worthy of this, and you will be rewarded. I will personally see to it that you get cold drinks after the first sale over a hundred today.

Rhonda walks away, looking satisfied. Ruth waits a few minutes then comments.

> RUTH
>
> What a jerk.
>
> JIM AND PETER
>
> Yeah.
>
> RUTH
>
> (picks up phone but does not call anymore)
>
> Listen, Jim... I want to talk to you. Pretend to dial out, you know? Hold the phone—but don't call anyone, okay?

Jim hits himself in the head with the phone by accident.

> JIM
>
> Ouch! Yeah, okay. What is this, a game or something?
>
> RUTH
>
> No. It is... I mean I want to know something.
>
> PETER
>
> (reciting lines to himself; he is exhausted)
>
> A lie I cannot tell. I lie and then... Oh hell, what is it about this line?

Peter puts his head on the desk.

Theodore, Roger, Marjorie, Marsha, and Mary sit together and snicker at the telemarketers, particularly Peter. They laugh and snicker in low voices.

Peter has now fallen asleep with his head on the desk and is beginning to snore.

> MARSHA
>
> Look at them... they can't even stay up to do their job. Oh, I wonder how well they would do in Pretonia.

Theodore, Robert, Mary, Marjorie, and Marsha laugh loudly.

MARSHA

Well, I guess some people are born with a chance, and they are usually not like those people. I mean, they can do something to improve their lives. When are they going to understand that not everyone is talented? And as we can see, they are just not in the bunch. Do you know most of them haven't even tasted the big time? But of course, that's pretty obvious, They're here, aren't they?

THEODORE

Well, sometimes they're in something, but you know, not anything important.

MARSHA, ROBERT, MARJORIE, MARY

Yes, that's true.

Rhonda comes back to table and sees Ruth facing Jim, and Peter, sleeping and snoring. Rhonda bangs her fist on the table and shocks Peter into an upward position.

RHONDA
(banging table with fist)

Must I be here every minute?

The vibrations can be heard on the desk.

PETER
(wakes in shock, sits up)

Oh my god—what happened? Where am I?

RHONDA

You're here, Peter, here in the world of reality. You will see me in my office right away.

PETER

I sold some group tickets tonight—about ninety people.

RHONDA

A job well done. I want to personally congratulate you for your performance tonight. Come into my office and I will give you a cold drink.

PETER
(wipes his brow and follows Rhonda)
And thank you, Ms. Inkwell.

RHONDA
(looks at Jim and Ruth)
What about you two? I hope you're not going to let Peter win this week's contest.

Rhonda walks away with Peter following her.

RUTH
Jim, now listen.

JIM
Okay, will this take long? I have to get a snack.

RUTH
Let's get this over with now. Are you born again and again? Or where do you stand on women? I mean... do you like women? Do you like me?

JIM
Well, you're nice, but you don't have enough hair.

RUTH
You like women with real long hair, huh? But that's not a reason to give up on me. I can grow my hair.

JIM
The police are wonderful, don't you think?

RUTH
Well, yes, I guess so. I have to keep believing that everything I hear is just an accident. He means, um, do I like police? Umm, umm, yes I do, when I'm alone in the subway. Actually, after my divorce twelve years ago, they helped me quite a bit. My ex had tied himself to the bedpost and I couldn't get rid of him. They knew how to untie a square knot.

JIM

I have been with a great many people—I thought I'd tell you that, Ruth.

RUTH

Are you saying you have one of those venereal diseases that just won't go away?

JIM

(looks like he's in another world)
I don't know what I'm saying.

RUTH

I am not going to cave in to a little misunderstanding. Perhaps he just broke up with someone. Perhaps everything is okay in the upstairs room.

JIM

Yes, the upstairs room is filled with desire.

RUTH

Oh, that's good, that's what I like to hear. Were you married?

JIM

No. Wasn't that restrictive on your swimming time? I'd like to be free to swim twenty-four hours a day—with time to be on land to make money, of course.

RUTH

(becoming resigned to Jim's lunacy)
I guess you're in treatment, too?

JIM

No, I don't think so. Lately, life has been confusing.

RUTH

I am in a species that is not growing upright. I'm not going to commit suicide like countless others. You can sort out those that made it through those days of hate by pinching them and seeing if they go into a world of their own.

Ruth pinches Jim lightly.

Jim speaks earnestly to Ruth.

JIM

I don't know who I am. I think I'm in the wrong body, actually. I like the smell of a woman. I like to pick at their earlobes. But I... I think I was meant to be a platypus or another animal that lives under the water. I'm thinking of a species change— like a lot of guys are. People usually go to one-celled animals, independent of all ties. I myself want to stay with the mammal in me but experience more rewarding pleasures.

CU Jim and Ruth. (close-up of Ruth and Jim facing each other, profile shots, heads of Jim and Ruth only.)

MUSIC UP from the downstairs performance area.

FADE OUT.

THE END

WHEN THE MARTIANS LANDED IN AMERICA

July 2010

A river is seen in upstate New York. Lights above the river move from a distance in the sky very quickly to just over the river. At first it seems to be an aircraft, but it approaches too quickly to be a plane. As a man pulls over to the side of the road and exits from his car to view this, the lights disappear. Then the UFO shoots a light into the river, moving straight up quickly until they disappear, again making no sound as they leave. As the man who reenters his car drives away, the lights reappear; a large UFO, cylinder-shaped, hovers over his car as he drives down the road. A light flashes into his car. He exits from the car, then the UFO moves quickly in a straight line upward and disappears. The car moves away. The lights reappear. The man in the car gets out and walks to a nearby police station in a small town. He enters the police station.

MAN. I would like to report a flying object which I am sure was not an airplane, which flew over my car, hovered over it, and released a light of some type.

POLICE MAN. Yes, we received at least one hundred calls tonight. Please sit down. An officer will take the report.

MAN. I would like to know if you have any background on what it should be.

POLICEMAN. No, I don't have any information. Please fill out this report, and one of our officers will be right with you.

A woman runs in to the police station.

WOMAN. Officer, a small green man is following me and he won't leave me alone.

POLICEMAN. Could you describe him?

WOMAN. He is very thin, about four feet tall, his skin is a frog-green color, and he has very small oval eyes. Very short eyelashes, in fact, I don't think he's a human being. He doesn't appear to be from our planet.

POLICEMAN. Are you saying he is an alien, a life form from another planet?

WOMAN. Yes.

POLICEMAN. Have you seen other aliens?

WOMAN (*said indignantly*). No, I have not. I would like to tell you something very important. He stands outside my house all night. He stands in the corner in the morning.

POLICEMAN. Do you work? How do you know he is out there in the morning?

WOMAN. Yes, I do. He is standing outside in the corner when I leave the house to go to work. He stands there. He does not move from the corner as I walk down the street to catch the bus.

POLICEMAN. Fill out this form. Someone will be with you shortly.

Lights flash into the police station. They appear to be coming from outside.

Two policemen run into the main room from two other offices.

POLICEMAN 1. What the hell is going on here?

POLICEMAN 2. Any reports from anyone who could tell us anything, Captain?

CAPTAIN. No. Although I wonder if there is anyone who could tell us anything if they knew what was going on.

If this is a screenplay, fade out, and the scene ends. If this is a stage play, lights dim or go out, or the curtain closes till the next scene.

In the same town, a bank is lifted from the ground and beamed up into an enormous cylinder-shaped spaceship. A few dollar bills drop out of the spaceship. People are seen on the street, staring at the spaceship in amazement.

A woman who is short in height with frizzy hair and a strong Brooklyn accent grabs the bills falling from the sky.

WOMAN (*grabs the money dropped from the spaceship as it reaches the ground*). God-d-d-d, money! I don't care, at least I could get at it. I suppose it takes an invasion from another planet to get my hands on a buck.

On a separate street, a woman who appears to be a street walker stands on a street corner. She stops another woman who appears to be a street walker.

STREET WALKER 1. Judy, did you hear about the aliens?

STREET WALKER 2. Yeah, it's something! I would have liked to do something like that. It would have saved me years of hell.

Two men leaving a bar look up and see a cylinder-shaped spaceship. They are drunk and speak in a slurred voice and have trouble walking down the street.

DOUG. Did you see that, Joe?

JOE. Yeah. It looks like a spaceship. I couldn't be having hallucinations?

DOUG. No. You don't drink enough to have that problem.

JOE. Hurry up, Doug. I don't want them to come after us.

DOUG. I can't walk any faster. I'll fall down.

The spaceship hovers over them. A white light covers their bodies for an instant.

JOE. (*looks up at the spaceship and talks to it*). Please don't hurt us. We are just two drunks. Useless people. We have no interest in life. We have nothing to offer you.

DOUG. (*looks up at the spaceship and also talks to it*). He's telling you the truth. No two people care less than we do about anything on earth. He never learned anything. I was the worst student in school all my life till I grew up, and I have no curiosity even now.

Camera moves to the inside of the bar near where the two men who are drunk are standing. If this is a stage play, the scene shifts to the inside of the bar. People are sitting at the bar, watching a news report on television.

Reporter on television can be seen and heard on a large television set at the bar. People are watching the TV set and drinking. They are listening and looking very anxious. The bartender is listening also.

NEWS REPORTER ON TELEVISION. People are advised to go home and stay inside their homes till more information is available. It appears to be an invasion of some sort. We have no information on who is behind this invasion. Numerous reports to police stations around the state of New York and a few from the Midwest are claiming that frog-green skinned colored aliens are following people, stalking them, hanging around their homes, and hovering over their heads. And a bank was lifted from its place on the street into a UFO today. A few dollars dropped out, and the bank, the entire building, and all the people remain aboard the UFO, which lifted at a fast pace up into the air and has not been seen since. An investigation is underway. It is a large cylinder-shaped UFO. People are advised to remain calm. The safety of all Americans is always of the greatest concern to our government, and everything is being done to protect us.

The bartender announces that the bar is closed for the night. The customers leave the bar in a very anxious state of mind.

This scene ends.

A woman is cleaning her apartment. She walks into the kitchen to clean. This is acted with great comic timing like the legends in comedy, Laurel and Hardy. She sweeps the floor and drops the broom several times. She finally steps on the broom brush, and the stick hits her in the head or body. She then picks up the broom and sweeps the dust into the dustpan and drops the dustpan, and all the dust falls back on the floor. To continue working and to relax, she turns on the radio.

WOMAN IN KITCHEN *(silently turns on the radio)*.

RADIO ANNOUNCER ON THE RADIO. This report just in. Aliens have been flying over the home of a general in the United States Army. General McArthur. Yes, his name is McArthur. The general reported he could not sleep and did not know what was keeping him up. He was restless, but did not know why. Then he looked out of his bedroom window and saw a cylinder-shaped UFO overhead, very large, about the size of a passenger plane. Then it lifted up into the air quickly and disappeared from sight, traveling up into the clouds in a straight line. No lights came from the UFO. At the same time, it is believed that it is unrelated. A volcano erupted in Iceland, causing six European nations to be affected with volcanic ash. Air travel is impossible in those nations. Airports have stopped all flights until further notice. Thousands of people are stranded across Europe, seeking hotels and attempting to communicate with those at home and at work.

Scene shifts to a man of color named William, who is walking in the forest in upstate New York and sees a large cylinder-shaped UFO hovering over the trees. The sun is setting. A beam of light hits him and he falls to the ground unconscious. No one is around to see this. When he wakes up, three aliens, four-feet tall are standing over him. They have little hair on their heads, soft fuzz. Their heads are very large, square shaped, and somewhat rounded. They have extremely empathic eyes, which are oval and small, And off-white skin color, almost the color of a white kitchen counter. The aliens who appear to be grays approach William. He moves away, gets up very quickly, and begins to run. The aliens look at him thoughtfully as though trying to decide if they should follow him. They decide not to and they reenter their spacecraft. William runs to the nearest town, which fortunately is less than a half mile away. He enters a diner, sits down, and begins to talk to the waitress who serves him.

WILLIAM. Do you have a phone? I have to call home. I just saw something. You won't believe what it was.

WAITRESS. Lately, just about every strange incident that could ever happen in a small town has happened. You can tell me. I would believe you.

WILLIAM. I saw three aliens. I mean it! Three small men, well, creatures with square heads, about four-feet tall, and small oval eyes. No ears or small ears, I don't know for sure. They were in a spaceship first. They landed and hit me with some kind of a ray. I became unconscious. When I woke up, they were standing over me. I ran away. They did nothing else and returned to their spaceship.

WAITRESS. That's amazing, but I believe you. Would you like a cup of coffee or a glass of juice? Something to relax you.

WILLIAM. I would like to phone my family.

WAITRESS. The phone is around the bend. Lots of stories these days. The news is filled with people seeing aliens. Of course, I believe no one really cares. After the excitement is over, things go on as they have. Aliens could easily take over. We have become so weak and disinterested as a people.

William finds the phone around the bend in the diner and phones his wife. He can be seen talking to her on the phone.

WILLIAM. Hello, honey. I'm so glad to hear your voice. Today was one of the most frightening days of my life. I saw three aliens while taking a walk. Yes, creatures from another planet. They tried to approach me. I ran away. I'm coming home. I don't want to tell anyone about it. I should see a doctor and be sure they didn't hurt me.

WAITRESS (*speaks to a customer*). He's smart to decide not to report what he saw. In the 1950s, the MJ-17 report, the government made on aliens looked phony. They were the ones I believe that released copies in the wrong bin in terms of its classification. They created a new copy. Years later, from a typewriter, which wasn't invented at the time of the report. It wasn't invented for another ten years, I think. If they weren't trying to cover up the facts, everything would have been in its proper place. Then they hire debunkers to write books on it. The guys they get to debunk it have the ability to list the facts they need better than the most brilliant lawyer, which is nothing next to cases where people claim to receive commands from UFOs. They could debunk a photograph that could not be mistaken for anything but a flying saucer with people from the Air Force, experts, to scientists that can make anything seem like a hoax.

CUSTOMER (*drinking coffee and listening to the waitress*). *Don't I know it.*

Scene shifts to a poetry reading in a café. A poet sits in a corner, talking to herself while the other poets stare at her. Her name is Rene.

RENE THE POET. I can't stand it anymore. Not every poet that reads confessional poetry is worth listening to. I hate even some better known poets I consider to be confessional poets. Why can't poets who talk about their experiences growing up sound like Christina Rossetti? "Goblin Market," I believe it was based on her life. It had an important message—that youth must never trust those that insist that they try what is being offered. Fruit by Goblins in this case.

IVAN THE POET. Who are you talking to?

RENE THE POET. I don't know, but they understand how I feel about good poetry.

POETRY HOST LOUISE. Quiet, please. I would like you to give your attention to Grace Love. Please come to the stage.

GRACE LOVE. Yes. A haiku by Laura Lonshein Ludwig.

Be selective, child.
In memory we live life.
A hand reaches once.

Be selective, child.
In memory we live life.
A hand reaches once.

Although some people may believe this is not a haiku because it refers to human beings as opposed to outdoor nature, trees, and flowers, a haiku can have people in the poem. People are part of nature.

IVAN THE POET (*talks to himself*). Yes, I am Jewish. Though I'm not religious. I relate to the culture by enjoying the many comics that came from my culture and the appreciation for the written word by many Jewish people, although I wouldn't call myself ethnocentric, unlike many of our current Jewish politicians. I remember our history and care about the feelings of other Jews and all Americans that respect the lessons of the Holocaust. Well, I know no one cares how I feel and what I do!

POETRY HOST LOUISE. Who are you talking to?

IVAN THE POET. I don't know. I heard a voice. It asked me if I'm Jewish and I said yes, but I felt I needed to explain to it how I feel about being Jewish.

At this point in the café, the room shakes, paper blows around, and lights flash in the room. The poets fall from their seats. The scene ends.

A new scene opens to a hearing, which is presented on C-SPAN television on NASA budget decisions.

SENATOR EGG. Are you seeking three million dollars for companies to control space exploration and research to work on the international space station?

MR. WASHINGTON. Yes. We have a great plan for our space station.

An assistant to Senator Egg stands behind him, laughing at odd times.

SENATOR EGG. The Mars Science Laboratory was hampered by technical difficulties and will be delayed till 2011. I do not think that giving millions to companies and firing NASA workers to start a commercial program would be fair. Research controlled by private industry, NASA should continue as it has and receive a budget for space exploration.

MR. WASHINGTON. The grays won't get in the way again. I mean, I have jobs for everyone. I feel safe and confident in my decision.

ASSISTANT TO SENATOR EGG (*smiles and bites his lip*).

MR. WASHINGTON. To help our crew, we must have workers. The space station will be over sixteen thousand pounds. We will be working on the space station, conducting experiments on humanoids for future use on the space station. Cooks and cleaners with no sex drive will have fur instead of fur-free humanoids. This is to see if fur helps reduce the burdensome curiosity that often gets in the way of working comfortably on menial tasks.

The scene shifts to the police station as seen in the beginning of the play. The same woman that reported that a green-colored alien was standing outside her apartment building is seen talking to the policeman also seen in the beginning of the play.

WOMAN. I would like to report that the alien that stands outside my house all night was in my house when I got home from work.

POLICEMAN. How did he get in?

WOMAN. I don't know. I locked the door and the windows.

POLICEMAN. Was it one alien or more?

WOMAN. Just one. The one I reported to you the last time I was here—the frog-green colored alien. He has small eyes, short eyelashes, and he's very thin and short, about four feet tall. I came home and found him sitting on the sofa. He was drinking a glass of, I think it was red wine, and he said to me that if I do not mate with him, he would place my name in Latin and my phone number on a wall with a description of the sex act I would be willing to perform for a price, as they did in Pompeii.

POLICEMAN. Was he drinking from one of your glasses?

WOMAN. Yes, from one of my very good wine glasses.

POLICEMAN. I understand. I wanted to fight crime, catch criminals. Have a seat. Someone will be with you shortly.

The scene ends.

A few miles outside a small town in upstate New York, Martians leave a flying saucer that looks like the flying saucers people imagined aliens would land in. It is saucer-shaped and large and has just landed in a field.

Six Martians leave the flying saucer. They look like the Martians people imagined they would look like in the 1950s, when people first began believing in aliens. The Martians have antennas on their heads, thin-shaped eyebrows as though they were made with a pencil line, and shiny outfits with no separation between shirts and pants. The Martians speak to one another.

MARTIAN NO. 1. The Earth is the easiest planet for us to live on, and they still have water. Volcanoes and floods left us with a cold, dry, empty desert and frozen water. Three hundred nine million miles, and at last we are here. After blocking the sensors on the Earth ship to Mars, we realized we could not stop all the others from coming to the planet. This problem will no longer trouble us since we will take over the Earth. At last, a home of our own, and we won't have to live in our ships outside of our planet.

MARTIAN NO. 2. Yes, it will be good to live here. I believe the Earthlings will help us. Everything is for sale here. It was easy to control the communication on the Earth ship, which was heading for Mars. We will have nowhere to go if they can travel to other planets. The barbarians love violence. The grays have studied them for years. The grays will help us. We can offer technology, drugs, money, and power. We discovered them through the airwaves. A box they call television, which they are entertained by, sent images of vulgar and stupid clownlike bursts of violence into space. They have selective vision, so it should be easy to give them choices that will interest them. They are competitive and unfair in the way they compete. We will take everything once we can confuse them enough to take control.

A woman walks into the field of dried grass that the Martians are on. She walks up to the Martians. She is carrying a pad and a pen and wears a button that says Register to Vote.

WOMAN. Hi, can I ask for a moment of your time? I'm conducting a survey. Are you registered to vote?

MARTIAN NO. 1 (*speaks to the woman conducting the survey*). We decide who will run for office and are the greatest contributors to the campaigns.

The End

FRANCE IN THE YEAR 1775

Written September 2014

King Louis XVI and Queen Marie Antoinette married not for love, but for affairs of state. Queen Marie Antoinette, who was once an Austrian archduchess, is very young and is speaking to the king in the first scene in the play.

QUEEN MARIE ANTOINETTE. They live in fear of taking a false step. I am sick of the minuet, the endless circles. Those horrible aunts and their knitting—hideous deceitful crones. This castle is filled with fiends. I long for Paris. I must find a way to leave Versailles. The Comédie-Française, the Italian Opera, the masked balls, the nights in Paris—that is what I desire. I am a young woman.

KING LOUIS XVI. Well, have a good time. I am not like you, Marie. I enjoy my solitude, sleep, wine, and a good book. I suppose Monsieur Leonard will work on your hair again. Hairpins, pomade, towers of hair. The very doorway in the palace had to be made higher so that the ladies passing through would not have to bend down as they pass. Your mother wrote to me again to say the newspapers printed that "the roots of your forehead rise as much as three feet and in fact are made higher by ribbons. Fruit, gardens, houses, ships in a storm, and the events of the day modeled with the comb on the summit of this pouf."

QUEEN MARIE ANTOINETTE. What a fuss Mother makes. Old people are so tiresome. Always preaching. I will get rid of my governess. A queen no longer needs a governess. Abb'e Vermond, the confessor and counselor Mother sent to me must be kept at a distance. Horace Walpole said to me something very important. That if there is any disharmony, the music must have been wrong, and that I did not dance out of time as I have heard some at court said I did.

Years later, the king and the queen are talking to each other in a very anxious way.

KING LOUIS XVI. There are more urgent things to consider now. This is a difficult age to rule in. All the wrong people have gained importance through philosophers like Voltaire, alchemists, necromancers, charlatans, and a line of people always forming for a place in your budget. During the twelve years I have been king, twelve hundred and fifty million have been borrowed. It is known that while the commoner works ten hours a day to earn a few sous, jewels worth a million and a half or more are lightly given as a sign of friendship. Palaces are bought for ten or twenty million while the people are starving. I tell you, Marie, I have been given a place in the world I never wanted.

QUEEN MARIE ANTOINETTE. I know you did not want it. You who do not like to talk to people would have been happier in a country house without a care in the world. I, too, was forced into this position by also being born into a royal line. I never wanted it. I always wanted to have a good time. Life can be so much fun. I thought as a queen, I could live as I wished to. The deceit I have had to fight has taken the advantages away.

A new scene in the sitting room in the castle. Count Axel de Fersen is the man Queen Marie Antoinette is in love with. This scene takes place after the king and queen and children fled the palace due to the storming of it by the populace, and the National Guard no longer fully defended them. They are now in a palace in Paris. Count Axel de Fersen and the queen, Marie Antoinette, may never have had full relations physically. They have been in love for years. A devoted friend to her, he is a handsome Swedish-born baron. He is tall of good built and has a tender smile. He is forthright and devoted in his attentions to the queen. After four years of voluntary exile to ease tensions and joining the American soldiers during the revolution, he remained in touch with the queen by letter. Now four years later, they are both thirty-four years old. Her hair is sprinkled with white. He has returned to comfort her. The queen is still beautiful. Now she is deeply depressed and concerned about her children's welfare and speaks to Fersen about it as he consoles her.

COUNT AXEL DE FERSEN. I am here to listen and help.

They hug in a loving embrace.

QUEEN MARIE ANTOINETTE (*to Fersen*). I am so worried about my children. Will we live through this? The peasantry, the army, the Jacobin Club, thousands are joining the revolutionary movement. Mirabeau can be bought. He's the National Assembly's most dangerous man. His demonic nature, he thrives on chaos. He can speak to people as no one can. He is a man that we would not want to have work for us at any other time, but the present, duels, seduction of women, lawsuits—he loves to make a great display of himself. That is his greatest love of freedom. He will work for us if we pay his creditors what he owes them. The king has promised him two hundred and fifty thousand. He is, now I hear, convinced that he no longer wishes to be at the head of the revolution, but he wishes to be an ardent royalist. He has said, "I shall be the champion of liberty as guaranteed by monarchial authority, my heart shall follow the road to reason." No one at the National Assembly is to know that he is advising me.

COUNT AXEL DE FERSEN. I am sorry you must have him help you. It is sad life has taken so much from us, and so much must be done to protect you, but you are stronger. Should you have lived differently, it might not have worked out this way, but we could not love as we wanted to—that would never change. I will always be here for you, loving you always.

The queen and the count embrace.

Months later, the queen speaks to count Axel de Fersen in a sitting room in the palace in Paris. They are alone.

QUEEN MARIE ANTOINETTE. Mirabeau is dead. He died from his nature, exhausted, serving us and the revolution to hide his intent. His excesses and his way of life killed him, always wishing to perform and making speeches in numbers not needed, planning treachery I did not think would work, and I did not allow him to do. Again, hanging diamonds on the necks of opera singers and women of less virtue. He slept with two opera singers the night he died. I have heard that a large number of people followed him to his resting place.

The count takes the queen's hand and they sit silently.

Months later, it is the summer of 1791. The queen and the count are again alone. They are speaking to each other.

COUNT AXEL DE FERSEN. It is arranged for you to leave the palace. This ride will take four and twenty hours. I have forged the passports for you. I have had your diamonds smuggled out of the palace. My guards will follow you on horses, hidden from the eyes of the people. You will have two carriages. The very best has been ordered with eight horses. The coachman and those brought to help will be trustworthy noblemen, of course. Food will be packed for dining—a silver dinner set and a wine cellar built in to the coach. Your clothes will be packed so that you can change from the common servant clothes you will be wearing. You will act as a governess to the children. No one will suspect who you are because Louis will be dressed as a servant as well, and the children will be with the two of you. They will be disguised. No one will be able to see who they are. Cloaks with hoods will cover their faces. The king stated that it would be better if I stayed behind and got away in safety to see that all is attended to once you have made your escape.

QUEEN MARIE ANTOINETTE. (*She embraces the count as she says this, with great sadness*) I will always love you. You have risked your life for me and for my children. You are the only real friend I have, and I cannot leave with you. If we do not see each other again, goodbye, my love.

The End

SHORT STORIES

The Lady Escapes to Rio de Janeiro

Written on August 2015

Some people are so cruel, they could incite others to murder. Some are so dangerous to the world, they could end all life as we know it. There is an equation to life and to the disappearance of civilizations. The hangman of hypocrisy spreads through the earth like water runs to the roots of trees. There are nights when the sweet scent of leaves brought thoughts of palm trees on a tropical island, a beach, waves racing to the shore. The white-lined waves raging higher in the rainy night.

I had to leave New York. I had saved for it. For years, I had wanted to take a boat ride to an island that was kind to those needing to get away. An island welcoming to the sensitive spirit deprived of a chance to live by an onslaught of repressive or harrowing events. I was reading a novel by Marcel Proust. Once, the characters reminded me of the middle class of the 1960s, living life to the fullest, though he was writing about the aristocracy of the nineteenth century. That was no longer true of the middle class of today. They are entering the life of the peasant of the past, seeking a place to make half-truths work in their favor out of fear. The news provided an incomplete account of all obstacles to restoring our rich and vibrant national identity. Tonight, I would begin to research the perfect place to go for a vacation and perhaps move to.

The water was almost a navy blue. People were having a wonderful time. Waves raced against the shore and children laughing ran into the water. Parents, calm and smiling, sat on blankets in the sand. A few people looked at a boat approaching—a small sailboat. I would dine at a good restaurant that overlooked the beach, sip cool drinks, and eat a crisp salad in the white stucco building—sharp straight, a hall to hear music in, a balcony, plants on the ledge, and stone floors. A restaurant in a building beckoned those to it, built by an architect renowned for his work. In the distance, I could hear a song I loved as a child, "The Girl from Ipanema." I was, at last, in the paradise I longed for: Rio de Janeiro in Brazil. I looked at the beach as I dined and the moonlight on the water. Someone was climbing on a rock to gaze at the sea. A woman joined him.

I would take photographs of the beaches, for I longed to have a memory of the peace and beauty I found at last. The city interested me less. The beaches, Ipanema, Copacabana, Flamengo, the soft breeze, the sunlight, the music of the country, the samba, and the bossa nova. Days spent swimming, nights reading in peace and quiet at last. I would not try to find out what it did not offer to the people who lived there. For that, I had sad memories of my own.

I looked out the window of my hotel room at the moonlight and saw a man approaching the hotel, a knock at the door and a letter delivered.

The End

THE GIRLS I GREW UP WITH

May 2015

We were a strange lot—friends with no real concern for the future, children who played together and became teenagers. We were always walking forward, for we were living in the soft breeze of mysterious endings, promised love, in long and unknown turned corners to new friends and unseen nations, boat rides, in a light rain, sun still peering through car rides to city streets we would someday take. Girls who longed for love, lonely when we had no boyfriends, thinking of the day when we would be asked to be the wife of someone we vaguely saw in our daydreams.

Shauna, Denise, and Nancy. Nancy, who felt comforted by Shauna as I did—who, because we were young and laughed easily and had time to be together, would spend hours talking, listening to rock n' roll, borrowing lipstick and eye shadow, excited about dyeing our hair.

We were not without strong beliefs. We had a loyalty that was fierce in a peace-love era, when hypocrisy was not tolerated and cruelty was shameful. I was the only Jewish girl in our neighborhood till I met one other.

I was not addicted to literature yet, to hours of reading great novels, later to become a writer while many of our friends became teachers from our blue-collar neighborhood.

When we walked through the streets of Brooklyn, it was as though we were in the most imaginative, exciting world. It was the precious feeling of freedom that gave life that special meaning. None of us had more than a few dollars, if even that, in our pockets at any one time. No one had a car, not even the boys, but adventure was everywhere.

Our mothers knew all the Broadway tunes, singing songs in the house, and I spent Saturdays and Sundays watching movies I would return to for a lifetime.

Christmas was spent at the homes of my friends. I received gifts placed under the Christmas tree and was loved like a family member. Life was lived fully. Older women went to the theater, loved to make dinner parties, ride bicycles, went to the beach, could swim for hours, knit sweaters, and sang while making dinner.

There is nothing like freedom to live without fear—the complete belief that you can find happiness by looking for it. No amount of money or the temporary delight of fame can be as wonderful or as memorable. We must return to this life again or we will long for it with broken hearts through the long, cold, strange, and cumbersome twenty-first century.

The End

A SHORT STORY BY LAURA LONSHEIN LUDWIG

My Journey to Ame rica
Written on December 2013

It has been said that from the beginning, America was a state of mind and not merely a place. Henry Banford Parkes described America that way in his survey of the American people. Though the colonies were not free of the forces that divided the people of Europe and some of the ideas that entered it were not the ones that would assure freedom. I left England to see what a young woman who did not have a title or much money could discover.

I would live in America with my aunt and uncle, my mother's sister and her husband. I saw much of them in childhood before they left for the colonies. They were very liberal and taught me Latin and Greek and had a great library in their house with the classics, which I read for hours.

I loved all of England. The birds flew over the church yard walls and shadows spoke to you. Words shared in small towns were precious, a sip of wine, and the promise in a stranger's smile slept with you and moved through your dreams. Holding on to the gains you made through work was not always possible. Europe held little promise for the commoner. After King Louis XIV died in France, the houses of the rich could be seen everywhere. The peasants were serfs in Spain, Poland, Prussia, and Austria. England now had changed. The rich merchant and the aristocracy were closer. The middle class had begun to see a chance. In America, the chance was greater. A person could acquire a farm without further payment to a landowner, or move to a town and, with some hard work, become a shopkeeper.

America did not grant that freedom to the Native Americans. There was never freedom for them. The Native Americans were imprisoned culturally when not murdered. Barriers were set in all the places where a life could be lived. Also, slavery existed in America. The black race was bought and sold and imprisoned on the land of those who took their freedom. This is what gave to America the question. Could America be an idea, a state of mind that was merely a vanishing road? Slowly disappearing from decade to decade without a deeply held philosophy to hold it in place. I had to leave the nation I was born in. Mother and Father were no longer there for me. Bringing my brother home, they vanished at sea. A storm shattered the boat. It was revealed to me at the dock. I was coming to a country that fought for freedom. It was hoped it would be offered to the people living there. George Washington, a leader and a soldier. La Fayette, a French aristocrat moved by the colonists' plight to free them from England. Rich merchants who owned businesses but understood it must be different from what the citizenry had suffered under a king, people who left nations that would not protect their freedom to develop their skills or allow them to develop their intellect and to pursue opportunities that would increase their earnings and ensure their families a secure future.

Tolerance of religious differences was to be hoped for as well. I was moving to a place where the Nyacks, members of the Canarsie tribe, lived. Native Americans who this land I was traveling to really belonged. These Native Americans were part of the Mohegan nation—a kind and graceful, welcoming people. They did not live (it was described to me) in tepees, but in longhouses. I was told before I left (by letter) that my aunt and uncle might be moving to Philadelphia within the year, where the founding fathers (as they were called) had made both law and competition a way of life for new arrivals, not always an inspiring competition. I have heard of their remarks about the elder Benjamin Franklin, the man of philosophy. I wondered if hard work and the building of new ideas also got the same attention, should they respect the needs of others. I knew that before independence, Benjamin Franklin realized the British would not deliver letters for practicing rebels. The congress elected him postmaster general for the American colonies. It is said that the triumph of the American Revolution for Benjamin Franklin would be virtue over vice.

I arrived in America in the summer of 1783, and I thought about the way it should be in America on the ship ride there. Would America honor tradition and life that worked well under certain conditions? Would they believe that a city is made through separation from one's first intention to an advance of a kind, to the decay that follows it, attempt to correct problems to more problems, leading to corrupt periods and reforms that could not last? Those who believed in this always got along well in business as writers, journalists, and artists. Citizens that went along with these changes were accepted. But would that end all respect for the value and beauty of the nature of the country if America had a weaker need for a culture that would define it as a nation than the countries in Europe? I arrived at the port. The sight of the unopened slave market sent chills through my body. I stood at the river's edge, feeling I had no reason to believe this place would be a home to me. My aunt and uncle greeted me. We walked past the sugarhouse, and my aunt smiles.

She says, "Here, more than a thousand soldiers died as prisoners of the British." There is sadness in her eyes. "England was where I was born. This is our new home, where we hope to build a better life. But there is slavery and so much more. I know you are thinking about it as you see the slave market. It is 1783, and the war of the revolution is over. Beth, it is so good to have you with us. We are so sad about the reason."

I embrace Aunt Pearl, whom I have always loved as a second mother to me. She was the one who chose my name, Beth.

My uncle stopped a coach. In England, the man who brought news from the town to the folks far from it, who was honest and reliable, was the stagecoach driver. He was as important as a captain of a boat at sea and was called captain out of respect.

"Captain," said my uncle James, "where can we find a tavern that local families like to have their evening meal in?"

"Smith Tavern right down the road," he replied.

And we had a good meal there. We are a family of vegetarians. We ordered a well-seasoned vegetable soup, rich in potatoes, and wine and cheese sandwiches with tea. On the same road, in a three-story stone house with a garden, roses were planted by the front door, and rooms for guests were available in the upstairs part of the house. The tavern keeper and his wife owned it and would offer it to families wishing to stay for a night or two. Our rooms were on the second floor. I had my own room with a good bed and blankets and a large window with lace curtains—which, when opened, let the moonlight in.

In a small room that was next to ours was a large tub. They brought steaming pots of hot water to us, and after we washed thoroughly and had a good rest, we sat down to have a talk in my aunt and uncle's room. Uncle James spoke about his concerns on where we should live.

"I believe a move to a farm far from people would be the best place to live. In this area not far from here, in Cherry Hill on the corner of Franklin Square, George Washington has a home where he lived in more often when he was inaugurated as president of the United States. John Hancock's home is at number 5 Cherry Street; and at number 27, there is a Captain Reid, who thought of the plan for the American flag. They live in mansions, and there are cherry trees that line the road. Many of the oldest and wealthiest families live there. Of course, there will always be those who try to build a nation and those who are wealthy without a moment's thought to the future of a nation, and some who may do nothing but ruin the very life they say they wish to build. Once we have too many people here and not enough jobs, there will always be an answer for those who can afford to leave, but we must find a secure home now.

"Some people have come to America because they would have died in prisons in Europe. Slaves are sold in Africa and in other parts of the world, and pirates from all over the world are on the waterfront. Near the river, there are some families that are the type of families I fear may begin to be seen more frequently. A man named Tom Hicks lives with his wife and two children. He is a pirate and works on a boat. He is believed to be a murderer, burglar, pickpocket, and works with others, I hear. His wife is a shoplifter while his son was involved in highway robbery. The daughter is thought to be an accomplice to a murderer; she has been seen on his carriage. Mr. Hicks came from the slums of England. He plasters his hair down and curls some of his hair when he goes to the tavern where he spends most nights with his girlfriends, who I hear work for him as prostitutes. I believe that he gets away with it because he gives some of his earnings to corrupt officials he works for. I do not know what his job is with these officials, but people like him would never have power in Europe. They enjoy it here.

"There are children who sell baskets of flowers to hide the job they do as a lookout for other ruthless men. They teach them the life of crime, sometimes kidnapping the small children. People are attacked near the river and robbed. Some very tough women are here, and of course, there are people who suddenly cannot survive. Poor souls. Some have become prostitutes to support children—widows from the Revolutionary War who cannot find work. I believe we have a better chance to secure our freedom and happiness by selling the store. To build a life here would require respect for the life of others, for the efforts of those who wish to preserve the best in fair dealing, respect for the dreams of others, a desire to see good business and family life, and protection for those without a family. This depends more on the character of those you live around than the exposure they have to a higher education. A true belief in democracy for everyone. Protection for everyone, not greed. The problems were brought to my attention by customers of the store that I sell fruit and supplies to. I would like to buy a house far from others in the countryside. You know we love you, Beth. You are like a daughter to us. On our land, we can plant vegetables. As vegetarians, we do not take the lives of the creatures of the earth. A cow can give us milk, horses to ride in the sunset. In our house, we can have a great library. I have all the books you loved reading and other classics, Beth."

"I can make clothes and help with the cooking and cleaning," I tell my uncle with great interest.

"Yes, Beth, you are a very good cook." My aunt Pearl hugs me as she says this. "And I am sure there can be a fine young man in your future, should you wish to marry."

"Love and the warmth of those who wish to see me happy—no other need is greater," I said as I embraced my aunt and uncle.

It is perhaps true that the decay that I see in this area is a political move that pays criminals to take the liberty from honest citizens while changing the beliefs of those growing up in this setting. Perhaps there is no place to live. I will continue to search for it. We moved to Pennsylvania in September. My uncle James carved the date we arrived—1783—on the top of the house, under the roof. The roof curved under it. He built the chimney. The tools to build the house were made by my uncle while we gathered the wood. Wooden pins were used in the framework of the barn and our house. I had a chest for my clothes with a large bird carved into it, its feathers spread. Our house had one floor. Uncle built the beds for the bedrooms. I slept in my own bedroom. There was much work to do; we were working for weeks. I made the quilts for the beds. It was night when we finished work on the cellar, which was used to keep our food cool. Wood shutters covered our windows, and we could hear the sounds of the birds in the morning.

One day, I sat in the sunlight. I saw a horse and carriage. The wind blew lightly and circled my knees. A young man passed, whom I would see again. Hope teases us and rests in our innocence.

The End

THE FIRST LOVE WITH LOREN

Written April 2009

The lonely, frightened man walked through the woods. Soft haunting woods, the forest, timeless in lost souls and boys hunted down by soldiers. This man was turning to a tree as though he wished to be protected by it, the cold bark. So many people want to find a place to go, wishing they could walk into the past, where each day was not so many random uncontrollable events, sometimes horrible.

It was late evening. He turned to look back and ahead, seeing nothing but the black sky in the woods. There was a man living at the house who would not leave. A relative of his wife's, or so they said. Strange things happened at the house—late night guests, sudden deliveries of bags, backpacks brought to him by men who spoke in a loud, tough, demanding language. Only a few words of each sentence could be heard downstairs where they slept. He was in the attic, insisting that was where he would have the most room and privacy. His name seemed made up. Tom Smith. How was he related? There was no one in Paula's family with the name Smith.

The agony of knowing he was the one that was not wanted, finding Tom beating Paula after a loud argument, and running to her only to hear her scream for him to get out. Beaten, shot at, and not able to return home. The police would never help. Heroine in the bags or jewelry or stolen money. He wouldn't say what was in the bags, but that Kevin would go to jail, framed for whatever it was Tom had done. Best to leave.

Rage moved Kevin to fight him and discover that his wife would help frame him for the crimes Tom committed if he would not leave. Kevin couldn't get the gun from Tom, and now his associates were going to find Kevin. He could not run far enough to escape them. The cars were coming all night. Each time a car drove by, fear covered his body. This is a different world from the one Kevin grew up in. No one hears or sees anything anymore. There is no way to tell who is involved in what he is doing. Tom said the local cops would never help.

Kevin thought about this, and also that the wooden people of the town who needed to be told each thing that is worth seeing would never help either. The rustling of the tree leaves frightened him. People came to mind. Tired, anxious-looking women whose faces begged for sympathy, who drew you to them, and, once given the chance, talked with excited pleasure about the murder of helpless creatures. Vacant-looking men who were capable of running prisons where people would be tortured, wiping out whole villages in a sadistic idiotic grin. Lost, lonely men who would find satisfaction in killing a man who also appeared to be homeless.

Life was nothing like the 1960s, even in the countryside. Nothing reminded him of his youth. Stupid violent movies, hateful, stripping the body of all reason to exist. Respect for the most artless fools when those that could recite Shakespeare, because of the great love they had for it, were easily crushed. Now with so little to hold on to, the one person Kevin trusted, his wife, had lied to him and tried to destroy him. He closed his eyes and saw his wife screaming, "Leave or you will be killed. Yes, I love Tom. I will protect him." The car was gone when Kevin ran from the house.

Dark shadows in the rings in the lake moved; creatures in the water could not be seen. A shadow of his face from the moonlight. Staring at the water brought a feeling of deep depression—ancient memories of desperate, helpless cruel endings and accidents. Exhausted, falling asleep against a tree, it was not until the sunlight warmed his face, raced into his eyes, that he woke. Anxiety returned.

Reaching into his pants pocket, he found a few twenty-dollar bills. Something had to be done. It was two miles to town. No one had followed him. He was only three miles from the house.

At the diner, he ate breakfast: eggs, toast, and butter spread heavily on it.

The coffee was strong and good. He saw a waiter he knew, and they exchanged a few words.

"Is that you, Kevin?" A voice—familiar, warm, sweet, once so loving, always trustworthy—was speaking to him. Looking up, he saw Loren.

"Loren, how very good it is to see you."

Loren looked lovely, as she always looked—sweet, beautiful, because her face was bright with kindness, gentle, wise, brilliant eyes, and chestnut brown hair. She was looking young. Though middle-aged, lines around her eyes added to the warmth. Around her mouth, only one could see some disappointment, caution, and that tired look that appears when asking questions from years of unexpected, sometimes cruel, experiences.

Why didn't he marry Loren? She was the woman he loved and trusted always. Her need to wait until they both graduated from college, found jobs, or went to graduate school, while neither of them graduated, money problems in a time of passionate idealism, endless delightful, intellectual curiosity, pleasure in each other stimulated by the insights they had. A perfect match, mind and body in delightful sensual, soaring discoveries. The long nights they sat talking about the world, philosophy, politics, literature, art, and music. The galleries they walked through on weekends. Dinners when he could scrape together the cash. Young and hopeful, waiting for their chance. In the present moment, painfully again, Kevin sighed. Lauren spoke to him.

"Kevin, I was visiting my aunt. I didn't expect to see you. You look so tired and upset. What is wrong?"

"Loren, you are not going to believe what has happened. What a fool I am, and it all took place in my house. I have married a woman that is dangerous, and I have nowhere to go now. She is involved with a criminal. He has done something, and they have been together in my house, running a scam of some kind with other people. She told me he was a relative. I regretted not marrying you for years. I blamed you always because you wanted to wait."

"So did I, Kevin. I regretted it always, though I would never say anything about it. You married and there was nothing I could do."

"Loren, I missed our long talks and the way we were together for years."

"Yes, Kevin, I know. And I never found happiness. No one who I could talk to or love the way I loved you. Kevin, you understood me. No one understood me the way you did. You understood my desire to get ahead, and you felt the same way. I wish I did not let it stop me from marrying you. We never finished school anyway. Money problems were always in our way."

Two men entered the diner and sat at the table next to Kevin and Loren. Kevin recognized them as neighbors, and when they saw him, they approached the table to speak to him.

"Kevin, I am sorry. Did you hear, or am I the first to tell you? I hope I am not."

"What, Paul?"

Kevin asked him with great fear, moving his body into a shaking motion.

"Kevin, your wife was shot dead by a man who goes by the name of Tom. The police said her last words were 'Tom, please.' Then he shot her. I was leaving the house to buy a newspaper when I was grabbed by a cop who moved me away from the scene by your house. Kevin, I am very sorry. I guess I am the first to tell you."

"Yes."

"Did you know who he was?"

"No, I didn't, Paul. And I don't even know what was happening between them. He was at my house, and she said he was a relative, though I don't think he was. Did they catch him, Paul?"

"Yes, they killed him while he tried to get away. They said he was a drug dealer and they were surprised to find him in this town. I am sorry. Anything I can do, Kevin?"

"No, thank you for telling me."

Loren and Kevin left the diner and decided to rest and talk at her house. They left the table, and after he paid the check, she looked into his eyes and saw a tear forming. As she took his hand, tears flooded into her eyes. This time, they would not let go, and nothing would keep them apart.

The End

LOVE FOUND AFTER WORLD WAR I

Written May 2016

War-torn towns in the forest, green lush, a Robin Hood's forest. The mountains, embracing years of war, leaves a lost woman broken in the madness of sorrow of never finding love to live in belief with in cabins with a perfectly set table by the fireplace. In times of peace dependent on the selective nature of mankind, which leaves so many without protection, the benefit of truth they are not honored with. Those who lost so much and often give more than their share, work to once again live life the way they were meant to. I read that ancestral spirits, sacred landscapes, and communication with the forces of nature are shared Native American attitudes. I also shared those beliefs. I was sitting by the fire in the wood-burning stove, a comforting corner of the room.

I was in town to buy a few groceries and to receive a message by telegraph at the general store. The sun peered out from the white sky. Earlier, it rained. I passed the watchmaker. I passed the train, which carried soldiers back from the war and were destined for the hospital. On April 6, 1917, America entered the war. I thought about those who died so young. Life is cruel. I thought of the wives and children and lovers now alone. I walked down to the hill where I left my horse and rode home wondering if we were pawns to those who used our lives to make money and gain power. The sun appeared in the darkened sky and then was gone. The clouds gray, a light rain, and it was gone. I was home before night fell and placed the telegram on the kitchen table. An old friend would visit with her brother. They were taking care of family matters—a house left to them by an elderly aunt. They would be moving close to me. At last I would not be so terribly alone. Lottie and

Daniel would arrive early in the evening. It was a rainy day; the wind chilled my arms and unfolded into the center of my back as I carried the groceries into the house. A lace-trimmed tablecloth. Plates and tea cups with roses painted on it, the print a bright red, beckoning you to enter the garden. Freshly perked coffee to greet them with, mushroom soup, salad, and since we were all vegetarians, a plate of pasta and a bottle of wine. Lottie looked tired when she stepped out of the horse-drawn cart, and we walked to the front door. Past disappointment, loss, in the corner of her eyes, lines formed, sandy-colored hair clung to her cheeks. Her good, loyal, and honest spirit gave her the type of beauty people with depth to their nature look for, for a lifetime.

Daniel had some gray hair, handsome as he always was. We were all a little older; middle-age was upon us.

"Ruth, it is wonderful to see you," he said.

We were all together again; how happy we felt. We had much to discuss after a good dinner. A few years had passed, sitting by the wood-burning stove, Daniel talked about the war and what they went through. They lost their younger brother, Teddy.

"I was too old to be in it. When Teddy was killed, we felt as though a good part of our lives were over as well, a sort of death in us. We were a family because of each other. There seemed no way to live life without our younger brother, who brought his innocence, curiosity, and wonderful playful nature to our lives."

Lottie said, "I was unable to live in the house, I took long walks. Dad and Mom gone too, the only bright spot in this was that they would never know their youngest child died before he reached twenty-three years of age. War is evil. I feel it could be prevented. Lots of games are played by the powerful men of the world."

Daniel spoke now. "It was, I think, about controlling the world market. Would America lead? The German people were starving, fascism spread, and the Jewish people were blamed by some. It was the beginning of an idea that has happened in history before. People forget that those that control the market are of many religions. Good people who contributed to the nation are suddenly seen as problems. Each nation has a religion, race, or type of person they will target. Some people fight in wars and never get what the nation should give them—rights to live with respect and opportunity. Brother wrote us about the problems those who are not white feel they face in our country, as he met men on leave who talked about it with him."

Lottie was deep in thought when she added another fact. "When Turkey and the Soviets were in talks, Turkey demanded not only the border of 1913, but also all of the territory taken by the Tsars since the 1870s. Terror-stricken Armenians fled, and genocide took place."

David said, "When the war was over in November of 1918, the Kaisers regime wanted the armistice. President Wilson was seeking a new place for America in the economic order. What would this mean for our future? There is nothing so precious as family. Even in this changed world, what does it mean to those who must face the cold and selfish nature mankind so often shows when an advantage is placed before them? Only in a truly moral world with a different philosophy from the one we have known would it make any difference. Friends and family are all we can really count on.

"Father found a better job in New York City, and I have stayed here holding on to our home, alone in the Catskill Mountains. You do not see people often, but like the city, there are problems. The nights are frightening and lonely." Daniel took my hand. "Ruth, we are here now, and our house is only a few miles from you. You will not feel lonely anymore."

I looked at him for only a moment. A warm feeling spread over my body, starting from my head to my feet, which felt like a schoolgirl's shyness. The week they arrived, Lottie was shopping for the supplies she would need to clean the house. They were going to paint the living room walls; a new coat of paint was needed. Daniel and I went for a walk on Saturday. The rain was, at last, at an end. It was a sunny day. We walked on the country roads hand in hand.

Daniel stopped walking. "I have a great feeling, Ruth, when I am with you, and it was strange that it did not happen before. You were always a beautiful woman, but I am attracted to you now. I feel a great friendship for you as we have always had, but I am attracted to you as well.

"I am feeling the same way, Daniel," I said, and we kissed. The sun warmed our bodies; the chill in the air gave us the spirit that is in the move toward the promising and exciting experiences in life. We walked till the moonlight made a path to my cabin.

The End

The Party in Manhattan

March 2015

Years will pass, but at some point in the week of any month, I will return to a night that was the entrance to the enticing life of the urban sophisticated set. I was in my mid-twenties, divorced at twenty-three. I did not know if I would return to college, though I loved it. A very good professor influenced me, and I dreamed of travelling the world as an anthropologist. The classics were my life till then. Teaching English Literature appealed to me. Working in Manhattan to take a break, living in Brooklyn, and working hard at a job in an office, I had little time and money to spend on going out. At last, an opportunity came.

In a large room, a party was given, created for people to meet. Single people roamed the duplex. Stopping at the table where wine and cheese were placed, people talked to one another. I was younger than many of them. They seemed to know about subjects I had little knowledge of—where the most interesting art exhibits could be found, the best restaurants, and bars where people in the theater discussed the shows they were in. One person worked at the United Nations while a businessman spoke of the problems in the stock market. The party was created by a woman who astonished me. Her hair was piled on her head in the most sensual and fashionable sweep. She wore a long white satin dress and had the figure of a model. She had a gold medallion on her neck, which fell into her dress. She was over forty years old. An older woman, I thought, a woman that looked that good and spoke with such eloquence and knowledge certainly was among the set of people that were truly cool. People moved through the rooms with drinks of wine or punch, sitting on a sofa with a knitted cover. The large windows let in the dark sky, and the apartment buildings in Manhattan could be seen. The night was wonderful. There was much to learn. It would take time. I was younger than almost everyone there. I left that night having met no one I would date. I felt inspired and excited to enter this world—to discover the world of artists and adventurers and to know more about business and to travel someday to the cities talked about that night. The evening and its promise stayed in my memory for a lifetime, long after I married the right man who I have been with for twenty-five years.

The End

POETRY

READING ERNEST HEMINGWAY

On His Life in Paris in the 1920s

When I think of Ernest Hemingway
I cry,
tears well up in my eyes
not for his sensitivity
he never seemed able to feel agony
for the suffering of others
that did not want more than to exist,
the way he could for a place or a reason in time
that must be saved.
The way he could see a painting
or the sunlight rise from the mountain top,
the separation of a man or woman
from their dreams.

His story
the fiction he wrote
was a call to embrace life.
The reason to reach it
not to wallow in the waste of memories
of unnecessary struggle
that so entertain those
that find no reason
to live without mediocrity,
countless reasons to fight passion
with every ounce of energy.

While some of us
cannot feel
that we are alive
without regard
to the precious moments spent,
and not really able when it is wasted
to spend our time now
walking through death
some would call a memory of life.

SEVEN DIMENSIONS

April 2011

I am in
Several dimensions
The houses
Are more alive than the people

In this dimension
More than the fourth dimension
It is in the nineteenth century
Or the early twentieth century
The house stands proudly
The wood doors live
In a calm sweet spirit
Of soft winds
In wheat fields

When the sweet scent
Of moonshine
Rested in time
The trees swayed
The corner of the barn
Stood firmly
Against the mystery of the night

Birds flew over it
For a century

After sitting on the porch

Writing a few pages of the play

I am inside again
Searching for
The next answer
To put a problem
In order

I wish for
The security of the past
And see
The green grapes
On my grandmother's kitchen table

Missing the security
Of easy-to-arrange order
In my life
And the feeling
That the future
Can be worked at
I search for a film
A classic
But I have seen them
Hundreds of times

It is better
Than a current film
Another possible truth
Though produced poorly
Aliens that rip
The heart of a man out
And have been doing it
To hundreds of people

Once it took a lifetime

To get close to your goals
Artists walked
Through the streets
All night
Sat at wood desks
By wide windows
Fresh paint on the door
To the theater
Rehearsing the part

The jazz musician
Stares at the boy
Whom he does not understand
And composes a new work

The devil in man
Punishes creative man

The puppet appears
Disappearing behind the mist
Then only the mountains
Could be seen

A WINTER NIGHT

March 2015

Trees in a row
Are left bare
In the winter
Ice falls from the branches
The wind races through them
I wonder do the trees
Feel abandoned
Longing for the leaves
And the warmth of the sun
The soft breeze
In a gentle night
Moves through
My body
The black sky
Has few stars
And the moon
Seems to study
The earth

The breeze chills
My body
With the promise
Of the mystery
In life
Moonlight places shadows
On the picket fence

And the garden path
To the house
Where reality hides
In the walls of the family room

Finding comfort
In those
Who love us
In the way mankind cannot, superior creatures
The dog and the cat
Comfort without compromise
They, too, seek the wonders
Of the earth
All we count on is truth
Perhaps human nature is judged
By the sun
And the planets above

A Cool Breeze in the
Sunlight of Civilization

October 12, 2012

The third eye is the intellect,
The soul, the blood of mankind.

The light on the lake
Is the measure of time.

When Monet
Sat on his boat
Staring at the water lilies, he painted.

Nature is in my love and I,
We run down streams
And are found in the roots of trees.

In L'Estaque near Marseilles,
Cezanne painted
The river,
The lines that divide time,
The mountain peak
Moving upward
The blue arrows of light, the life of man.

Perfect lines in the distance
Between a mountain
And a river,

Small houses
At the bottom of the mountain
Where we rest.
The boats move in the wind,
They are in their place
Waiting for us to enter it.

The landscape painter
Enters the studio
The sunlight moves through
The painter's small cluttered room
As he paints,
One wonders,
Is not art love also?
The romance in the painting.

Time and place
Is everything in life.

Born to a time
When playful carefree
Days as a child
Climbing trees
Sitting by the flower bed
Inspired the poetry Robert Frost wrote
As a boy,
Or to a time
When there is no place to compose.
Or to a time
that inspired hope.
Edouard Villard's
Oil painting on a panel.
"Interior With Figures sewing,"
Carmel and burnt orange,
The black design

in the orange table covering
You could feel the cloth
As you look at the paining.

As a child
I remembered those colors
In my maternal grandmother's home.
Though she did not have
Much formal education,
And could afford only the necessities in life
She shopped for affordable supplies for me
And prepared a table for me
Each afternoon after school.
And on weekends as well,
A table with pencils and art pads
And notebook paper,
Watching me draw and write
With love in her eyes.

Looking at a child
Speaking to his father today
I thought,
What a flower of a mind children have.
Though innocence is discovery
We are born to a time and place
That keeps alive
The beautiful child in us for life,
Or takes the child from us in our youth.

THE NEW CENTURY

Written June 2015

The waves rolled in
The ocean lonely
For the passion in men
That walked by its shore

All that gone
When there was no place
To make a home

The dictator left his seat
Angry to lose the chance
To bring to a close
The life of the citizens

For centuries somehow
The sun
And the moon
Rise again and again

Romance was in the air
The stars filled the sky
The sweet scent of leaves
Beckoned one to think
Of the mystery of love and life

The night was like this
When I felt neglected

By those I counted on
When life was threatened
Even when the death
Of the most beautiful soul
Take place

Romance must have been in the air
Before men walked the earth

JAZZ

August 2016

There are the beautiful stories
In the trees
Standing in a row
Of light rain
The flowers
Speak to me
In Louis Armstrong's jazz

Down the dark alley
In time
They held each other tight
Sipped drinks
Looked into each other's eyes

That joint was jumping
That world was jumping with life

There was art form
Delight in creation
Rooftop parties
Doors opened in the summertime
There was hope

Ethics is philosophy
Chivalry
There was a will to change
Though the world was always tilted

And those who created real liberty
Punished as in any other time

The loner understands
Hypocrisy
Is the undoing of the future with it

In the desert air of New Mexico
There is always the longing
Of D. H. Lawrence
And Mable Dodge
And Frieda speaking of him

The past is always with us
It peeks through
The sunlight
In the trees

On the highway
The ancient mystery
In the grand design
Through the soft wind
In the dark night

The crickets
Speak the language of suspense
In the countryside
Where the pleasures in life
Should take
Long sweeping strides

The firefly
The eternal childlike delight
In a sky filled with stars
My husband
Saw a shooting star tonight

ALTERNATIVE UNIVERSE

July 2012

White fence
Moonlight behind it
The grass seems to go on for miles

Lifetimes of grass
Behind white wood fences
The lights are promising
Mysterious, they move me
Through the garden

The garden that calls to me
It is the one
With lights
That moves through it
Like arrows
In the direction
Of that life
I could have lived
Where I am
Creating films that are
The full turn
The complete purpose
Of my art

The camera is turned to
The mountain
Where I danced

Toe pointed
Leg perfectly straight, raised
Like a ballerina
Dancing in delight
Because a film
I created is complete

It had close-ups
Of an actress
In shadows
Shyly tilting her head
By a stone cottage
Breathtaking
She speaks
In a soft voice
Beckoning to those who see her
To the director's lifelong search
For what is memorable, great in cinematography

She is like Ingrid Bergman
Perhaps the only one
And I have captured
Her timeless beauty
Her sincerity
Words spoken slowly
To her lover
In the film
Moon inside her rounded lips

The camera shifts
To the light of the moon on the ground

The films I would have made
From the plays I wrote
And would write

Walking past the garden
I see the universe
The alternative universe
That I could have lived in
If it had worked the way
I hoped it would

I pass by a boy in the town
The boy looks tired and distracted
His father looks sad but smiles at me
His eyes thank me for my concern

A DRIVE IN THE COUNTRYSIDE

August 2014

The delicate violets
Chilled by the wind
In the corner of the slanted sunlight
Trees on both sides of the road.
The scent of leaves
In and out of time
The rain must fall.
Like Nino Rota,
The music in *La St rada*,
The film by Fellini.
There were roses in my aunt's garden.
I wondered what it was like
To live in a heaven on earth.

Like a child entering a fair
The shadows forming a line
I still wait for a chance in life.

On a lazy summer day
I ache for the timeless desire
In childhood.

The houses seem to fall beneath the trees
As they stand without a person left in them.

Driving in the countryside, my husband, Ray, says,
"The perfect summer

Was the year I was five years old
And my sister was talking about boys,
I was playing and no one had an interest in stopping us."
I think of my childhood,
Once when my skin was
Like moonshine and honey.
The moonshine covered my body
And I believed
There was nothing
But mystery
And sweet enchanting days
Before me.
But it was too often interruption from these things.
Like Nino Rota,
The symphony from *La St rada*,
The music is the pace and strength
And gentle moments.
The chase is life
Which is a circus
Of tightrope walking
And deceit
Though often is saved
By devotion and sincerity respected for the many not the few.

A WRITER'S LIFE
April 2015

A light dimming
Under a round red glass shade
On a lamp
In a room
Long ago
Like one perhaps,
E. M. Forster passed nights
Working on a novel.

A lover leaves a room
And a chill is felt
The rain falls lightly on such nights
The darkness outside is a romantic force.
The wind lightly rustling
Against the window pane
Blinds shut.

Writing The Longest Journey in 1907
E. M. Forster contemplates with Lytton Strachey
And Virginia Woolf
What life is, in time.

The shadows appear
With a different awakening
A lamp sits on a table
In the corner of the entrance
In the study

Books stacked
A pile of papers.

On the boat
The writer remembers
Walking in the east one night.
The black sky
A few stars
Incense, the scent of mint and ginger
The leaves burning.

Ancient quest
In reincarnation
Only morality
Leads us forward.

THE FORCE IN NATURE

July 2015

It was on an island
Where everyone owned
Their light, passion and cruelty.

The sky was gray blue
They were wealthy and driven by myth.

Heartless Pandora leaves one man dead
Who took his life,
Unloved by her, and one man
Alone who she promised to marry.
In a trance she dives into the ocean

To follow a boat.
Pandora was a woman
Who had many lives.
In this one she found
Love and empathy
When the ship went down.

Our memory of belief
Was in long looks at one another
Flowers painted on tea cups.

In our passion we
Fell into an embrace
So immediate,

Loved easily, passion swept us
Into love.

Longing for nights like that again,
When for years were intruded upon.
Last night you held me in your arms,
My darling husband.
Your passion was not unlike
The love we felt
For one another,
Years ago.

THE LOVE OF MY GRANDMOTHERS

March 22, 2016

Swimming to the shore
Of a myth
I understand those
Who swim in muddy water
And breathe heavily
Reaching the street
With no light
Where no one wishes
To see you succeed

The dream can slip
Through your fingers
Then there are friends
I will miss for a lifetime
They loved with a purpose, sincerity

To be loved with a pure love
The purest love
I return to the love of my grandmothers

In a moment
I am in an apartment
On the bottom floor
Of a house
My maternal grandmother lived in

She spoke Yiddish and English

In the bedroom, a dresser
With a box of face powder on it
And a string of imitation pearls
On the table a radio
We listened to

Towel dried
After a soapy bath
She held me in her arms
I slept so soundly
There were no books on her shelves
Little formal education
A fear I could not understand
With all her heart
She wanted me to find my path

Both grandmothers bought art supplies
Pens and paper

Antiques and art books
Cluttered the apartment
My paternal grandmother
Was a teacher
She smiled proudly
At the remarks I made when she took me to the ballet
Living on a small pension
There was always money for new books
And art supplies

On my wedding day
At the party
She made to celebrate it
Her face warm with happiness she held me close
That is the love I ache for, for a lifetime

A Confessional-Styled Poem by a Woman from the Working Class

February 2012

There is something in a man that's in his soul
That shines out of his intelligence.

In a parallel universe,
in a cool stream of air
that moved through
our moonlit garden,
crickets chirped
in nights of quiet reflection.
We were happy in our home
every night was like the first few.

We gazed at the pear tree.
I drank cool drinks under it.
The lilac bushes drew us to them,
perfume in the air.

Summers we looked at the stars,
it was like the garden in a Fellini film.

The quiet of the country
made it easy to age slowly.
Our passion became greater
as the years passed.

This was not what happened.
What happened was quite different.

More than three decades ago,
when I was twenty years old,
I visited a teacher.

I walked through her pantry
to see herbs,
and flowers
that she picked in the forest.

We were in college
to be the best guardians
of democracy.
It was the end of an
idealistic era
in America.

Sitting at the dinner table
in a white wood enclosed porch,
the window to it opened
to let in the fairy tale fragrance
of her garden.
Invited to dinner,
roasted turkey, mashed potatoes,
butter streaming from the top of the potatoes,
I was not a vegetarian then.
Coffee, peach pie.

In a work-study program
in the kitchen of our dining room
at college,
I worked as a dishwasher.
Cleaning the dishes

for the two hundred students
at Franconia College,
a private school.

I could remember Mother,
who was sad, lonely,
disappointed with the life she found
once she was on her own again,
abused by her boss at work,
though proud to have a job.
My mother could type eighty words a minute.

Mother was gifted,
she sang like an opera star,
drew pictures,
the faces of people,
never using a magazine
or a photograph
to work from.
It was so good
it seemed as though
she studied art.
A smart woman
who did not go to college
and might not have graduated
from high school,
struggling to make ends meet.
This was more of what I knew
in the world
than the great possibilities
my educated loving grandmother

on my father's side
offered to me.

In college, I stayed up nights
writing papers for class.

My professor
a young determined woman,
as I see her now,
gave me courage.

I came from the city.
Our high schools did not have
large private pools or any pool.
Shakespeare was not offered
though we read
some good American playwrights,
in our courses in literature.

Girls did not have a basketball team.
We did exercises to improve our waistline.

We rode to school on the subways.
Rats crossed the tracks,
the other passengers,
tired looking adults
on their way to work,
hoped we would keep quiet.
We did since they looked so angry.

College was different, it was fascinating.
I took a course in Cultural Anthropology.
I hoped to go out on digs some day.
I planned to study
Physical Anthropology

the following year.

Instinct versus culture,
sex and aggression,
warlike cultures,
gentle respectful cultures,
My professor opened the door
to the wonders of the world.
That year she thought
I might make a good professor someday.

Nights without sleep,
writing papers for class
in an intellectual trance
rolling paper and a tobacco pouch
in my pocket.
Rolled cigarettes were too
expensive to afford.

Years later my husband
gave me a reason
to quit the habit
of smoking cigarettes.

In the city
I read the classics on the subway platform
till I was too tired.
I worked as a secretary, then a saleswoman
in customer service, but I wanted to work
as an actress.

Acting classes,
auditions for acting roles

but sadly the reason
I had entered into it
had disappeared.

The film industry
was moving further away
each decade
from the golden and silver age.
This was a political direction
for a nation
that would not support
a soul-searching population.

There are more tales to tell.
Some are horrid
that I will not reveal
in this poem.

One truth was constant.
Each year America moved further away
from the great intellectual,
artistic, inspiring,
idealistic, nation
it was when I was a young woman.
The saddest change is the lack
of respect for honesty.
I often think I simply grew up in an
idealistic era.
One thing is certain, the nation
that I live in now is like another nation,
it is nothing like the one I grew up in.

THE FALL SEASON

October 2012

The trees stand thin stately narrow and tall
The orange leaves on the trees
In the beginning of the fall

Nature is perfect
In color it is beautiful
In sight and sound
The clock within it
That moves summer orchid scents
To orange leaves
To cool dark night
Where the birds still seek
A place to rest
In the moonlight

The ancient poetry of the universe
In the accident of nature
Rocks in the waterfall
The strange place
Mankind finds himself
After so many centuries
Nature is perfect
Without the intrusive predator, mankind

Poking at its beauty

Leaves on the grass
I thought of those
I will always long for
Long gone
While so many are here now
That make life bitter and hard
The night when the sky was black, gray
With a purple light the stars in a line
Not a house light was on the road
Only the wind could be heard
In the first night of fall

RAY AND LAURA WATCHING THE MOVIE LA DOLCE VITA

May 2011

Like an ivy plant
Hanging over a stone wall
Hiding the unknown
Mysterious fated
Meeting place

The bubble breaks
In a champagne glass
Or is it the sound
Of the cork
Exploding
As the champagne bottle
Is opened

The father, who is my age
Explains to his son,
That he can show him
A thing or two about life in
La Dolce Vita

I know he is saying this
Because he must prove
We are still
In the passion
Of life

As we get older
And we are

I have touched my husband
And he has touched me
With the desire
That a Federico Fellini
Film inspires

I don't think
About the tension
In the film
Love that cannot work
Incurable obsessions

Candles and mirrors
Wing-tipped cars
Anticipation of love
Adults free enough
To be children

A time machine
Would be dangerous
When will it be
Like this every day again
In the world we must
Live in?

BIOGRAPHICAL NOTE ON LAURA LONSHEIN LUDWIG

Ms. Ludwig has been listed in *Who's Who in the World* for the last six years. She is a screenwriter, actress, poet, director for television and radio, and producer of a top-rated television show (*Earth Is Not on Tape*) featuring the artists of New York, both the rising stars and those renowned stars that have produced the greatest contributions to American art—from talk-show host Joe Franklin, the *Joe Franklin Memory Lane* show, who brought the actors and singers we have enjoyed and learned so much from, now seen on the Turner Classic movie station and other stations, bringing our greatest heritage to us in film and stage. The legendary comic Professor Irwin Corey appeared on Laura's television show, enjoyed on stage on Broadway in the play *Sly Fox* to a film produced by Woody Allen and countless other stages presenting his hilarious comedy. Al Lewis, legendary comic actor, enjoyed in the *Car 54* television series and movie, appeared while running for governor in the state of New York; and Bianca Jagger appeared on Ms. Ludwig's show during the Kosovo conflict to alert the audience to conditions there. She is the former wife of rock-and-roll legend Mick Jagger. She offers her warmth and concern as an activist, following in the tradition of community television on BCAT. Laura remained true to the concerns of her viewers, a Christmas concert at the Trinity Church, the New York poetry circuit, comics, opera, ballet, and presented other great hosts to talk about the work they produced, such as the host and producer of *The Light Show* on WBAI radio 99.5 FM in New York City, an arts and music show. Laura's goal was to create the type of television that would bring the standards back up to the great television and movies she loved in the best years of television production for today's audience.

Laura's TV show ran from 1994 to 2002 until Laura moved to upstate New York, where she currently hosts a reading at the Inquiring Minds bookstore in Saugerties, New York. Ms. Ludwig is a recipient of four New York State Council of the Arts awards from *Poets & Writers*, received while working with the Museum of Sound Recording, producing shows recorded on equipment used by legends in the music business acquired by the president of the museum, Dan, who produced tapes from the shows. Some of Laura's books can be found in the Mid-Manhattan Library, New York University, Bobst, Film Library, and libraries around the world and in good bookstores in upstate New York and in San Francisco, California, in City Lights Bookstore. All the books can be ordered by your local book publisher through the websites ***www.xlibris. com***, ***www.amazon.com***, and ***www.bn.com***.

The author of six books published by Xlibris Corporation, you could phone to order. Call 888-795-4274 or 7876. Each book has plays for the screen and stage. Some have short stories, a novella, and all have poetry. The books are *Robo Sapiens*, *Sounds Like a Plot*, *Reflections for the Renaissance*, *The Haunted House and the Stolen Gold*, *Gulliver of New York*, *Turn Out the Lights*, and *Memorable Plays and Short Stories for the Screen*.

www.ingramcontent.com/pod-product-compliance
Lightning Source LLC
Chambersburg PA
CBHW031512120626
46545CB00005B/1846